Hollywood's Top Dogs
THE DOG HERO IN FILM

Hollywood's Top Dogs
THE DOG HERO IN FILM

by Deborah Painter

Midnight Marquee Press, Inc.
Baltimore, Maryland, USA

ISBN 13: 978-1-887664-84-4
ISBN 10: 1-887664-84-X
Library of Congress Catalog Card Number 2008926647
Manufactured in the United States of America
Printed by Imagine Printing
First Printing by Midnight Marquee Press, Inc., May 2008

Dedication

To my sister Pamela Painter,
who does more to improve dogs' lives than anyone else I know

Polish one-sheet poster for *Benji the Hunted*

Hollywood's Top Dogs

TABLE OF CONTENTS

ACKNOWLEDGEMENTS

The following persons made significant contributions to this book: Lance Brown, member of the family of director Lawrence Trimble; David Hawk, interviewer and film scholar; Michael Ramsey, film scholar; Jere Guldin, UCLA Film and Television Archives film preservationist; Daphne Hereford, Editor of *Rinty's News*, a publication of the Rin-Tin-Tin Fan Club and the ARFKids Foundation, Incorporated; Kathy Wittwer, historian of the German Shepherd breed in film; Debra Marshall and her amazing animal actor, "Opus"; Michael Curry, director of the American Theater in Hampton, Virginia; Allan Shields, historian of Rin-Tin-Tin; Lee Harris, dealer in rare films; Mark Layne, video production company president and computer problem solver; John Kenneth Muir; Dan Condon; Karen Lauderback; director Joe Camp; Forrest J Ackerman; Pamela Kinney and Pamela Kay Painter.

The following organizations also helped in the preparation of this book: Sinister Cinema, Grapevine Video, Movies Unlimited, Warner Bros., Universal Studios, the UCLA Film and Television Archives, Sony Pictures, Paramount Pictures, the American Theater, The Hampton, Virginia Public Library, California Polytechnic State University and Old Dominion University.

FOREWORD

This book is no encyclopedia, though its value as a reference is significant. Writers on film history, as well as readers, will need to start with Deborah Painter's rich research results in the future. The legacy of her dedicated study will be permanent in the literature. Moreover, her writing skills, developed over the years, enhance the reading pleasure.

Important from the reader's standpoint, the author's insistent focus on her carefully circumscribed and defined viewpoint on the movie dog hero will hold the reader's attention. The result is an attractive narrative account of over 100 years of canine hero movies. This is no mean achievement, given the extent of the original, scattered resources. Simply dropping a few names of your friends and mine helps to suggest her coverage: Strongheart, Jean (a very early star), Rin-Tin-Tin, Peter the Great, Asta, Flash, Lad a Dog, Lassie (a dog), and Benji. The mere listing of early and late actors reveals the long-range coverage of the text. This fascinating roster of leading males and females (and one cross-over), whose admirers are legion, argue *prima facie* for a rich story—and the reader will not be disappointed. (It is of interest to note that the most frequently cited actor-hero ["Woof!"] in the Index is my virtual pal, Rin-Tin-Tin. There: Full disclosure!)

Two early writers on movie canine stars discussed in the book are Lawrence Trimble and J. Allen Boone. Lawrence Trimble is rightly given attention for his pioneering animal movie work and his enormous gifts for handling domestic dogs, as well as wild

Every kid wanted their own Rin Tin Tin button.

wolves, not to neglect his own writings on movie animals. J. Allen Boone's three volumes should be read and reread as a trilogy in which he quite deliberately and courageously abandons any diffidence or fear of anthropomorphizing Strongheart, and lets his devotional love and understanding pour forth. Worth mentioning also is the major theoretical, psychoanalytical work on animal films by Jonathan Burt, a British writer, discussed in Deborah Painter's text.

Perhaps one had to have been born about 90 years ago to feel the impulsion of those early flicks. I was born in mid-1919, while Rinty was born in 1918, and so I grew up as the sagas of Strongheart and Rin-Tin-Tin emerged *seriatim* from New York City and Hollywood. Thus, Rinty and Strongheart were virtual (but real) pals of an enormous audience of kids and not a few of their parents who were also (reluctantly?) drawn into the thrall. Still, in 2006, when Benji and Lassie are approaching their own mythical status, new canine idols on leashes and off will once more grow from tumbling puppyhood to mature, national stardom. Quelle dogs!

In the end, after reading Deborah Painter's professionally crafted and written work, we may all feel the nostalgic reminiscences she shares leading us to say, with a certain human actor, "Thanks for the memories..." At least we can Hope.

—Allan Shields, author, *The Spirit of Rin-Tin-Tin*
Emeritus Professor of Philosophy
August 24, 2006

INTRODUCTION

The history of the dog hero film contains all the excitement and appeal of any successful motion picture narrative. There is high drama, as in the tragic story of the meaningless accidental shooting of a canine legend, Peter the Great, at the height of his popularity, and the well-publicized trial that followed. There is glamour, which we see in the extensive roster of "who's who of the motion picture industry" actors, directors and screenwriters involved in the dog hero genre. There is altruism, as in the fascinating story of the director who was inspired by his work in training canine actors to go on to become a charter member of The Seeing Eye, Inc. There is an ethical framework, as seen in the history of Benji and his producer, who uses the fact that the animal actors in the films were adopted from shelters to promote the attractiveness of adopting pets from these sources. There is sadness, in the realization that many films in the dog hero genre are probably gone forever, existing only as paper ephemera, color slides and other memorabilia. There is artistic appreciation, as observed in the work of film preservationists who retrieve the sometimes tattered remnants of our shared film heritage and make the films available for future generations.

Elizabeth Taylor, Clara Bow, Richard Dreyfuss, Alfred Hitchcock, Darryl Zanuck, Chevy Chase, Tom Hanks, Gary Cooper, Bruce Dern, James Belushi, Clark Gable and Madeline Kahn have at one time or another either written, directed or performed in a dog-hero film. These super talents often began their careers with such films, or even made a career of canine cinema.

Films such as *The Doberman Gang* (1972) and *Dracula's Dog* (1978) portray the canine species in a less than favorable light. This book does not seek to analyze the above cur-villain thrillers, nor will the author focus attention upon talking animated dog heroes such as the main characters in films like *Balto* (1995) and *All Dogs Go to Heaven* (1989). The author considers films like *Because of Winn-Dixie* (2005) to be fantasy films because live animal actors are "morphed" using computer generated imagery so that they move their lips to form human language, or

TV's *Lassie* starring Tommy Rettig was really must see TV for kids of all ages.

smile. Any behavior or feat that could never be part of a real dog's repertoire, such as flying, smiling, speaking, reading or doing martial arts moves, is the stuff of fantasy films. Films featuring robotic dogs and dogs from other planets are best left for analyses of the science fiction genre. This book celebrates the dog hero motion picture wherein live, non-computer enhanced dogs engaging in heroic acts are either important protagonists or the primary focus of the film.

The dog hero has existed in motion pictures for 100 of the 110 years of cinema and in televised media for a little over 50 years of its 70-year history. At times, the dog hero genre in the United States and other countries appeared to have faded out, and nearly a decade passed with no significant canine hero on the motion picture or television screen. Then a new form of the dog hero emerged—because the subject, like most genres and sub-genres, is subject to cycles. The cinematic canine champion itself is a figure emerging unexpectedly from marginal characters to play a crucial role. Strengthened by the existence of living, non-fictional dogs displaying altruistic behaviors, the genre is one that will endure.Many people have asked me why I selected this particular topic for a book. Surely, they commented, many similar books have been written. There have in fact been books on individual dog stars. Two books were published about Rin-Tin-Tin, two on Strongheart, two about London, one on Benji and even one about Peter the Great. To my knowledge, however, there has not been a single book prior to mine on the actual subject of dog heroes in film. And, even though a number of books have been written on dogs and cinematic animal stars of all species, all but one, a work by Jonathan Burt, have approached the topic in a carefree and humorous style, as though the authors were embarrassed to be caught writing a book on animal movie stars and had to make amends by injecting satire and laughing at the animals. The books even included ani-mated animals like Walt Disney's Pluto! The general consensus among books,

periodicals and documenta-ries on the subject of film appears to be that animals cannot act and thus are not suitable subjects for serious film discussion.

I take issue with the as-sumption that animals can-not act. I have researched the careers of many dogs and have read interviews with their directors. I have also observed the dogs them-selves in their film roles. Some of those dogs were really acting. Many of them displayed the emotions I expect to see in dogs. They

On the set of *Marlie the Killer* (Photo courtsey Rae Mal-neritch and The Old Corral)

emoted toward their human co-stars in a manner that would be more in keeping with the way they would naturally respond to their beloved owners. I have seen Higgins, the dog in the original *Benji*, appear frustrated on camera, looking utterly defeated, walking alone down a sidewalk after his failure to get the FBI to pay attention to his urgings to follow him to two kidnapped children. I have seen Rin-Tin-Tin place his front paws on a kitchen table and cut his eyes first at June Marlowe and then John Harron, looking at each longingly as though pleading, "tell me what I did wrong." I have also seen him hungrily salivating over fellow actor Walter McGrail in *Where the North Begins*, convincing me that he wanted very much to eat him. Seconds later, his appearance softens in a single take and he stops salivating and snarling and then begins to lick the man's face as he lies in the snow. Later in the film he embraces McGrail as though he was his best friend in the whole world. If that is not acting, what is it?

Many people have told me that they love *Old Yeller* and watch it many times and cry many times. They are responding, they say, to the way they feel about their own much loved pets and how they would feel if they had to have them humanely destroyed.

This book is for these people, those folks who either have a dog or who would like to have a dog. The love of a dog for its human friends is pure and

simple, as is the love these people feel toward their four-legged friends. People want to see this on the screen and that is what the best dog movies supply in abundance.

As the years pass experts predict fewer and fewer lost films will be redis-covered because of nitrate decomposition, which can progressively destroy old films if they are not carefully preserved and archived. However, since beginning this book in 2003, it seems a wonderful coincidence that prints of films such as *The Love Master*, *Tracked* and *Sign of the Claw* have been discovered in Europe or in the Library of Congress and have been successfully preserved. Movies I thought I would have to travel hundreds or thousands of miles to see are being sold by mail order companies! Unfortunately, this alone does not assure us that these films will remain available to the public. If there is not adequate interest in buying these titles, there will be less of an impetus to distribute and sell such films.

Forrest J Ackerman is a name familiar to many baby boomer fans of classic science fiction and horror/fantasy films. He has made a career as an author, editor and archivist of our film heritage. In the 1950s through 1970s he was one of a small corps of writers who extolled the virtues of fantasy and horror

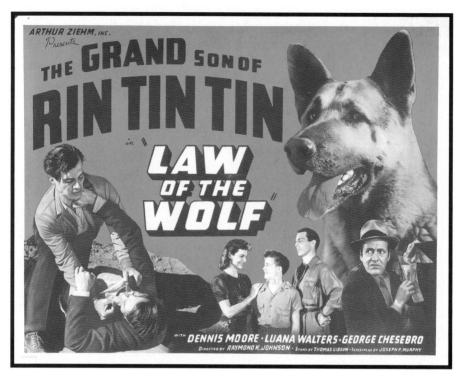

ARTHUR ZIEHM, INC.
Presents
THE GRAND SON OF
RIN TIN TIN
in "LAW OF THE WOLF"

WITH DENNIS MOORE · LUANA WALTERS · GEORGE CHESEBRO
Directed by RAYMOND K. JOHNSON · Story by THOMAS GIBSON · Screenplay by JOSEPH P. MURPHY

films starring names like Lon Chaney and John Barrymore to a whole new generation of fans. Television stations of the day either did not show their films at all or aired them on the late, late show. Prints of the more obscure titles often survived only through sheer happenstance. Young readers of his magazines and books were assured that these actors and their films were excellent and that the young fans should make a point to see them and help assure their preservation. "Lon Chaney shall not die!" was a popular expression of Ackerman's.

Well, to me, "Strongheart shall not die!" is my battle cry. And neither should Ranger, or Lightning, or the several Rin-Tin-Tins that we have seen in films and television over the decades. They are still capable of capturing our hearts with their canine charms. So the next time you're looking for some inexpensive family entertainment, go online and check out some of the websites

38. ''Strongheart'' takes a few minutes off for play while working in the Canadian Rockies.

Strongheart cards given away with Shotwell candy in the 1920s

Hollywood Walk of Fame stars honoring two of Hollywood's Top Dogs Rin-Tin-Tin and Strongheart

at the back of this book. The technology of today will bring these charming old classics right to your door and the microwave will provide you with the essential bucket of popcorn as you and your family snuggle down for an exciting and heartwarming night at the movies (that is also easy on the pocketbook). Spend some quality time with these daring canine champions whenever you get the chance. You will remember them all your life.

CHAPTER ONE

THE WORLD WAR
AND THE DOG HERO

The closest and most cooperative companions of man from the ranks of the animal kingdom, who share our planet are the dog, the horse, the cat, the dolphin and the elephant. Not surprisingly, these are the animals that form the bulk of the animal heroes of film. Admittedly, Tarzan's chimpanzee cohorts figure in close to 200 jungle films from 20 countries, but in real life, one would be hard pressed to find more than a few dozen wild chimpanzees that would oblige humans with their willing companionship. Dolphins and elephants seem naturally curious about humans, and the partnership between the dog and the human is much studied and celebrated. Dogs, cats, elephants, horses and humans are so close that it seems impossible to imagine that they would not be important protagonists (and occasional antagonists) in film. Dogs and trainers are relatively abundant, and the canine species is easy to train and capable of athletic stunts as well as having good memories and being versatile performers.

Dogs and other animals have been depicted in world cinema since its very beginning. In Jonathan Burt's insightful book *Animals in Film* (2002), he discusses film historians' offhanded dismissal of their depiction in film. One would think that any movie that had an animal as its main protagonist was automatically assumed to be a film of no consequence. Burt cites his difficulty in even finding references to animals in books and scholarly treatises on cinema.

1895's *Boxing Cats*

Index after index lists "animation" but not "animals." [1]

Animals were actually among the very first cinematic subjects in such short films as *Boxing Cats*. From the 1895 *Boxing Cats* to the 2005 *Dreamer*, animals are commonplace as secondary characters, set pieces or even as modes of transportation. This reflects the real world in which the audience members dwell. Domestic

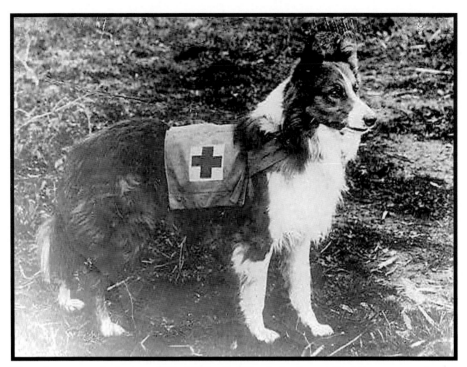

Many dogs were also heroes of World War I. This photo shows a Red Cross rescue dog in Italy. (Library of Congress)

animals such as dogs are not only a part of the landscape or cityscape but also an integral part of life.

The sagacity of dogs, their simple and honest emotions, their fidelity and the courage they show in defense of their puppies or their human friends, is real and undeniable. We ask so much of dogs and they ask so little in return of us. Early on filmmakers realized the dramatic potential for this fact of life.

Dogs were used in World War I as Red Cross rescue dogs for their ability to pick out the dead from the living on the battlefields and help lead the Red Cross workers to the living soldiers. A number of breeds were used, including border collies, but the predominant breed for this purpose was the German Shepherd dog. The breed itself was relatively new, having been established in 1909. Dogs were used primarily for work until the early years of the 20th century and the years following the World War. America and other countries settled down to rebuild and to pursue peacetime aims. The middle class in America began to grow in number and importance and with it came a surge in the popularity of domestic dogs, whose only function was as companion. Books and magazine articles devoted to the heroism of dogs in wartime and humanitarian work also found an audience. "Balto," an Eskimo dog, was lauded in print for his work as the lead dog of a dogsled traversing a distance of 660 miles to Nome, Alaska in horrific weather during the diphtheria epidemic of 1925, bringing life-saving serum to the town. The world famed Iditarod race commemorates that trip.

Balto, however, did not fare as well as his fame, ending up as a live exhibit in a roadside zoo.

Albert Payson Terhune, author of *Lad, a Dog* and dozens of popular magazine articles glamorizing the doggy exploits of Fair Ellen, Wolf and a number of his other collies, was among the first writers to benefit from the dog hero trend.[2]

In the early decades of the cinema, dog heroes were made to appeal to all age groups. Rin-Tin-Tin alone saved Warner Bros. from the brink of bankruptcy, and went on to star in about two-dozen films. This could not be possible if his films appealed only to children who went to the theater during the matinees, or their parents who went with them to see the pictures. The dog hero films in the 1920s and 1930s, unlike the films of the 1950s through the 1980s, occasionally dealt with adult themes such as attempted rape and murder. Animals routinely attacked and killed other animals and occasionally even killed antagonistic humans. The older dog heroes were all working dogs or dogs raised by wolves. No matter how wild the animals were when the film began, they proved as steadfast and loyal as any loved pet who had been cared for all its life. In many of these films, the dogs were the most intelligent animals the audience had ever seen, and thus the films cannot be said to depict utter realism, but can't the same be said of the vast majority of action/adventure films of the early 21st century?

Gratuitous violence in the 1920s canine films was very like the majority of action films beginning in the 1970s. Inept, crooked law enforcement officers and dishonest politicians were the rule and not the exception in these early dramas and we still see these same archetypes in entertainment today. The late silent and early sound films tended to be populated by adults. Some featured children and babies inserted to provide heightened suspense and pathos. After 1940, the protagonist/human heroes in the films were mostly teenagers and children, although there were some exceptions (*Eyes in the Night, Sergeant Mike, K-9, Call of the Wild: Dog of the Yukon*). In contrast to the dog hero films of the first three decades of cinema, the films after 1940 depicted fewer spectacular stunts, which was in keeping with the changing standards applied to humane training

BIG BOY WILLIAMS and
WOLF HEART

and treatment of animals in motion picture production. Animal actors no longer had to run until they were exhausted, or walk along the crests of huge dams, as they had in the earlier decades of filmmaking. Scripts were tailored to accommodate new ethical standards for animal training and handling. The majority of modern filmgoers insist on these standards. The scripts, unfortunately, often fell victim to overly sentimental and predictable storylines that failed to keep the interest of filmgoers over the age of 18.

Some aspects of the dog hero film did not change. The first six decades of American film usually demonstrates an exemplary dog with better than usual senses of sight, hearing, smell and intuition. He or she has an uncanny ability to track down his or her human friends' scent, even if many months have passed and the canine champ is exceptionally noble and intelligent, often taking matters into his or her own paws, but sometimes realizing the need for human help. The perspicacious pooch has difficulty getting humans to pay attention when warning them of danger, or trying to lead them to a hidden document or a person in trouble, but realizes how important it is to get their attention and communicate. The audience feels the frustration of the animal and rejoices when the dog is able to finally convince the humans to help save the day.

THE BLESSING OF THE ANIMALS

TRUE STORIES OF GINNY, THE DOG WHO RESCUES CATS

PHILIP GONZALEZ AND LEONORE FLEISCHER

"Philip—and Ginny—have done it again. And I've got a secret for you. Much as I loved the first one, I love this one even more." —Cleveland Amory

Occasionally, dogs in the real world (rather than the reel one) perform heroic acts that show amazing intelligence and sacrifice equaling, and sometimes exceeding, feats of fictional canines. Such incidents often make the news headlines. For example, a small pale yellow mongrel dog in Chinnakalapet, India, made international news in late December 2004 for saving the life of a boy. The dog, known by its human friends as "Selvakumar," was aware of a coming tsunami. Its seven-year-old master wanted to enter a small shed near the shore to escape the waters and the dog, seemingly knowing that this would prove fatal, pushed and shoved the boy to higher ground.[3]

Another renowned heroic dog, "Ginny," of Long Beach, California, had the unusual trait of risking her own life to rescue cats and kittens from grave danger. On one occasion, she dug through a box of broken glass to get into a warehouse to save a trapped kitten. Ginny, a Schnauzer-Husky mix, died in August 2005 at the age of 17. A heroine to 900 cats, Ginny is the subject of two recent books, *The Blessing of the Animals* and *The Dog Who Rescues Cats*.[4] Sometimes life really does imitate and even outdo art.

The first three decades of world cinema were the time in which it flexed its muscles, explored the various genres established by the stage and by literature, and found its economic strength. The dog hero genre was highly adaptable to film. Many of the films in the genre were Westerns, some detective films and war films. Later they moved into the family drama subgenre.

The first dog hero of cinema was a collie named Blair who retrieved the baby of an affluent family from Gypsy kidnappers in the seven-minute British film *Rescued by Rover* (Hepworth, 1905). This film distinguished itself by being one of the very earliest to be edited in a manner that introduced the main characters and important plot points efficiently

Rescued by Rover **(1905)**

all the way to the climax. The first German Shepherd dog hero in film was Dick the Detective Dog, who engaged in heroics to bring his master's killers to justice in the five-minute Pathé film of 1909, *The Nobleman's Dog*. A Husky dog named Baree saved its Native American heroine from an evil trapper in 1918 in the lost film *Baree, Son of Kazan*, produced by one of the very first female filmmakers, Nell Shipman and her husband at the time, Ernest Shipman.

Pioneering female filmmaker Nell Shipman with her cast and crew filming in Idaho.

The Dog Hero in Film

Strongheart started the longest dog hero film cycle, which lasted from 1921 to 1931. Husband and wife team Lawrence Trimble and Jane Murfin, co-founders of Trimble-Murfin Pictures, recognized the trend early and became the first to exploit it in motion pictures. Lassie, Benji, Ace and all other film and broadcast dog heroes had their predecessor in a famous German Shepherd. The name of the dog was not Rin-Tin-Tin, but Strongheart. Strongheart was the first dog hero who was actually groomed for stardom. His director and, for a time, owner, was Lawrence Trimble, who got his start with Vitagraph Film Corporation. Vitagraph was a very prolific studio, producing most of the short dramas and comedies of the early 1900s. Jean, a collie, starred in several comedy shorts where she spent much time rescuing and generally entertaining children. Lawrence Trimble and his dog came into the motion picture business at the right time for them.

The lanky redhead was born in 1888 in Robbinston, a small town in Maine. He moved to New York City around 1908 with his collie, Casco Jean, in tow. His goal was to be a writer. That year, he sold a story about animals, and the magazine sent him to interview the Vitagraph Company and write an article on the new technology of filmmaking. Vitagraph had a studio in New York at that time. Trimble and Jean happened to show up on the lot at the same time that they needed a dog to play opposite their star, Florence Turner. She went to work

Hollywood's Top Dogs

and did so well that Vitagraph hired both her and Trimble. He negotiated a salary of $25 per week for her and signed on as a director. Trimble also found favor with Turner, who wanted him to direct all of her movies after that. Vitagraph was the first major film studio and the first one to have stars. Rex Ingram, Norma Talmadge and John Bunny are famous names from its heyday. Jean appeared in *Jean Goes Fishing*, *Jean and the Calico Doll*, and *Jean and the Waif*, among others. Most of these were filmed in Maine, which proved to be a prime location for films made on the East Coast during American filmmaking's pre-Hollywood era.

Jean

That era ended around 1913, when studios started their exodus west. Jean died in 1916 and for a while, Trimble tried to use another dog, Shep, as a substitute. Shep did not have the same box office magic as Jean, so he went on to work for Thanhauser and became "Shep, the Thanhauser Dog."[5]

Trimble decided to have another try at a hero dog, this time for features for his own production company, Trimble-Murfin, which he co-owned with Jane Murfin. He asked friends where he might be able to obtain a suitable dog. They put him in touch with Bruno Hoffman of the Protection Kennels in White Plains, New York, who had purchased a police dog from a German officer impoverished by the War. No longer able to even care for his charge, the officer had shipped him to America. The animal trusted no one and Mr. Hoffman did not know what to do with him. Trimble recalled in his book, *Strongheart, The Story Of A Wonder Dog* (Whitman, 1926), that he was convinced the dog was suitable for motion pictures because of his and Jane Murfin's first meeting with him:

> We had gotten about 20 feet inside the fence when there came a
> sudden crash of glass and a hostile growl and Strongheart came

though a front window, glass and all, and was tearing across the lawn at us…Fearing that Miss Murfin might make the effort to return back to the fence, I shouted. "Stand Still!"…under the stress of the moment, I said it loudly, distinctly and most earnestly, and it had a very unexpected result. Strongheart took it as a command intended for him—and he stopped still.…If either of us had moved, I knew he would have resumed his attack. We stood facing each other for some time…I decided to see if I could not instill further confidence in him that we were all right. I said, "Here," and indicated with my finger a position at my right. That is the position of a police dog with respect to his trainer.[6]

Etzel von Oeringen, born in Germany on October 1, 1917, had been trained since puppy hood to be a police dog. He was descended from Norès von der Kriminalpoletzi. A huge example of the breed, weighing in at 125 pounds, Etzel had lightning fast reflexes and seemed completely vicious. He was not a wild animal; he was merely trained for one purpose.

Trimble bought the dog for Miss Murfin. Strongheart, as he was renamed, began his new training. Having never had the chance to enjoy the spontaneity of play, he was placed in the temporary charge of young boys who showed him how it was done. [7] In the evenings, he lived with his caretaker, J. Allen Boone. Boone was a journalist friend of the Trimbles whom they entrusted with their dog when they were traveling. Later, the large dog's training for the films began.

Strongheart's first role was as "Flash" in the film *The Silent Call* (1921). This screenplay, written by Hal G. Evarts, has Strongheart emote as Flash, a half-wild dog in the Canadian wilderness that has a wolf for a mate (a real wolf, Lady Silver).

Flash only trusts one human, pretty Betty Houston (Kathryn McGuire). He ends up having to rescue her from the miscreant of the film, who has tied her up. The time honored dog hero film phrase "Go bring help!" originated here. Jon Provost as "Timmy" in the *Lassie* television show uttered a variation of this command many times over the course of that series.

In the process of trying to blow up a mine entrance, a criminal seals off a den full of Flash's and Lady Silver's puppies. The death of his pups aggrieves him deeply, but he knows that he saved the girl's life. [8] A tearjerker

ending such as this one only assured stardom for the huge dog.

Next was *Brawn of the North* for First National. In this Jack London-esque tale, Strongheart was "Brawn." His co-stars were Irene Rich as Marion Wells, Baby Evangeline Bryant as "the baby," and Lee Shumway as Peter Coe, the father. The film is lost.

The Love Master had Strongheart portraying a sled dog that helps his young master, David (Harold Austin), who wants to enter a dogsled race and win some much-needed money. Lady Julie, Strongheart's real mate, was "The Fawn." This film was presumed lost until the Archives du Film du CNC in Paris, France, announced in 2005 that it had discovered it in its film vaults.

Strongheart was the first movie dog to be on the radio, giving a "speech" on WOR in Newark, New Jersey, in 1924, following a celebrity appearance with Lady Julie at the Westminster Kennel Club.

FBO (Film Booking Offices) Pictures, the ancestor of RKO Radio Pictures, released *White Fang* in 1925. Theodore von Eltz played the hero, Jack, in this long lost film based on the Jack London novel. Von Eltz had a Brendan Fraser quality. Ruth Dwyer was Mollie Holland. Strongheart was the noble savage in this film, according to his biographer, J. Allen Boone. He replaced the noble savage Native American so common to motion pictures. Strongheart proved himself a director's dream. The many fan letters received by the dog during production made it clear that they expected him to *be* White Fang. One scene required that he allow a bulldog to best him in a fight. He had never backed down to any dog before in his life. However, when Trimble asked him to allow the bulldog to "beat" him, the former attack dog complied. [10]

Strongheart worked on the presumably lost film *North Star* in 1925. Released by Associated Exhibitors, it was directed by Paul Powell from a story by Rufus King. Howard Estabrook produced North Star and Clark Gable had a bit part as "Archie West." It was his first film role.

Strongheart's only readily available film is, ironically, not typical of the genre of films that made him famous. Most of his other film titles, *Brawn of the*

STRONGHEART & JULE
IN "THE LOVE MASTER"
TRIMBLE-MURPHIN PICTURE

North, White Fang, The Silent Call, The Love Master, and *North Star*, take place in, well, the North. *The Return of Boston Blackie* (I.E. Chadwick, 1927) is a jewel caper set in an urban environment. Boston Blackie films began with the now-lost *Boston Blackie's Little Pal* in 1918. Blackie was a jewel thief who was constantly trying to put his criminal past behind him if anyone would let him. He found that someone was in constant need of his services for opening safes. In *The Return of Boston Blackie*, Raymond Glenn (who used the screen name Bob Custer

in his Westerns) is Boston Blackie. After a prison term, the thief vows to reform. His aged friend Rob (J.P. Lockney) and faithful dog Strongheart do their best to help him. Rob has rented an apartment and decorated it with Blackie's furniture earlier placed in storage. Blackie keeps getting entangled against his will with an old compatriot in crime, Denver Dan (Coit Albertson), and his blackmailing ring. Denver Dan owns the Mayfair nightclub, where he employs Necklace Nellie (Rosemary Cooper) as an operative to have affairs with wealthy married men and persuade them to give her baubles. To help save the family from the errors of her philandering father, daughter Sylvia Markham (Corliss Palmer) yanks the family diamonds right off the neck of Necklace Nellie. Blackie witnesses this, and, misunderstanding her motive, wants to keep her away from the police and convince her to stop this life of crime before she ends up in prison. First, he has to take the jewels, get her in a cab and send her away. Fleeing from an officer, the man and dog board small biplanes in an amusement park swing ride near the ocean. To separate himself from the purse containing the jewels, Blackie puts the handle in the big dog's mouth. "It's up to you to make the jump!" The dog then performs a daring leap from the ride into the waters off the amusement park pier. He then swims ashore and goes home with the purse. Blackie is shot by the officer and escapes to his apartment. Strongheart, not

understanding what has transpired, goes off to steal food. Denver Dan goes into the apartment and steals the necklace back. Sylvia has followed the dog, and she and Rob summon a doctor for Blackie.

Sylvia needs Blackie's aid in returning the necklace to her mother's safe at home. "I'll do it tonight. It will be Boston Blackie's last job!" he tells her. Blackie makes an unexpected visit to the Mayfair nightclub and intimidates Denver Dan into giving him back the necklace by pretending to have a gun in his pocket. Unfortunately, Denver Dan is as smart as Blackie. As the young man looks on, Dan calls the police. "This is Markham. I have it on good authority that someone will try to steal jewels out of my safe tonight and I would like to ask you to place some of your men on duty here." Dan's plan is to grab the diamonds from Blackie when he tries to return them.

Strongheart has a net dropped on him by sausage vendors. They shut him up in a shed and carelessly throw a cigarette in it. Strongheart crashes through the window of the burning shed, pounces on Denver Dan at the most opportune moment when he runs out of the suburban estate with the necklace in his pocket, and wows the local police force.

Strongheart's major job in this film is to be the sturdy helper to Boston Blackie, who is trying to keep as far away from criminals as he can, but a pert "criminal" catches his eye. The dog is able to detect bad characters by using that intuition that almost all movie dogs have. Strongheart barks ferociously at Denver Dan when he first appears in the film. "Strongheart doesn't like you," Blackie tells Denver Dan, "and from now on, I play his tips!" Strongheart takes the stolen necklace from Blackie's possession when he is being chased by a police officer, and carries it to their apartment. He provides a little comedy by stealing sausages from street vendors, but this is not a mere gag; it is essential to the story that the dog run afoul of the vendors and be trapped in the shed so he can escape it in a spectacular way in the very nick of time to help Blackie. In the final reel, he is a hero. We all know that had he not been able to follow his master's scent and dashed up to the front yard of the Markham home at the precise moment that Denver Dan is sneaking off with the necklace, the Markhams would lose everything. That was an admittedly far-fetched plot contrivance.

Variety's reviewer did not care for the film: "Assisting in the labors for justice is Strongheart, the dog actor. The casting is not good and is shown to poor effect in a weak brand of photography….the low type of audience will, as usual, derive some entertainment from this."[11]

Weakheart is a character in animated shorts that satirized the popular dog. The creation of a young Walter Lantz, Weakheart is the companion animal of a mischievous boy by the name of Dinky Doodle. The comical canine bears no actual resemblance to a German Shepherd. Weakheart looks more like Oswald the Lucky Rabbit or Bosko or one of the dozens of other cartoon characters in vogue at the time. Apparently, few *Dinky Doodle* cartoons have survived the ravages of time. Jere Guldin, film preservationist with the University of California Los Angeles, provided this book with information about Weakheart.[12]

Strongheart's human co-stars liked him because of his ability to avoid leaving marks on his victims. He might tear their clothing very nearly to shreds, but he did not harm them. Strongheart's intelligence, physical prowess and wonderful disposition captured the hearts of Americans. Suddenly, thousands of people wanted a brother or sister of Strongheart, and so Lawrence H. Armour of Lake Forest, Illinois, imported Strongheart's father Nores von der Kriminalpoletzi to the United States. The dog sired several generations of German Shepherds, but breed fanciers did not like his short tail, so the line discontinued by the 1940s.[13]

Strongheart's last film is listed in the 1928 *Film Daily* Year Book as *The Warning*.[14] The film is apparently lost and there are no existing lobby cards, stills or scripts known to remain. The dog star died at the age of 12 as the result of a tumor that developed when he was accidentally burned by a hot studio lamp that fell on him in 1929 during a fight scene. The author has been unable to locate any documentation regarding the set where the accident took place. His death was announced in many of the major newspapers of the day. Since Strongheart never made a sound film, he is not seen on television, and *The Return* of *Boston Blackie* can be seen if one buys a DVD or video from mail order companies or catches it at a film festival. Fortunately, the recent discovery of *The Love Master* in France gives younger generations a chance to see him in his younger days. Of all the canine heroes, he, Lassie and Rin-Tin-Tin are the only ones to have stars on the Hollywood Walk of Fame. Strongheart's star is at 1724 Vine Street.

Lawrence Trimble went on to become a charter supporter of The Seeing Eye, Incorporated. He and Jane Murfin divorced. During the decade of the 1940s, he married the daughter of the co-owner of Vitagraph. Trimble died in 1954 at the age of 66. Jane Murfin found greater fame and fortune as a screenwriter for acclaimed films such as Constance Bennett's first major film *What Price Hollywood?* (1932). Murfin died in 1955 at the age of 63.

STRONGHEART, DOG MOVIE STAR, DIES AT PACIFIC HOME

Los Angeles — (AP) — Death has called Strongheart, canine film star, from his retirement.

The first dog actor of the screen died yesterday at the home of his owner and friend, Jane Murfin, who brought him here from Germany eight years ago. Strongheart was 13 years old and had been in failing health for several years. He under-went an operation three months ago.

From the battlefields of the World war came Strongheart, to win for himself a measure of affection from the followers of the then silent screen. The dog had received his preliminary training in the kennels of the Berlin police and had served with the German Red Cross during the war.

Miss Murfin, playwright and scenarist, brought the animal here and introduced him in the movies. With his first picture "The Silent Call" Strongheart attained success. The picture was a signal for a mad rush to Hollywood by masters of his canine brethern.

Others of his pictures were "Brawn of the North," "White Fang," "North Star" and "The Love Master."

One of director Lawrence Trimble's relatives kindly shared some information about his family. Lance Brown, a Melrose, Massachusetts, native, is a distant cousin. Mr. Brown has spent most of his life in Maine. Lawrence Trimble was Mr. Brown's paternal grandmother's first cousin. His grandmother died before he was born in 1964. "Unfortunately, there are no family stories about Mr. Trimble and his famous dogs," said Mr. Brown. However, he has some knowledge from other sources about the beginnings of Mr. Trimble's

Strongheart

career. "He left Robbinston, Maine, to pursue a writing career in New York City. The story I read was that he decided to take a break and take a walk with his dog Jean through Central Park.

"At this time, New York City was the movie capital of the U.S., and there was a crew filming a movie. The crew was having issues with a dog that had been trained to perform in a scene. Somehow, Larry Trimble was either asked or offered to let his dog Jean perform the scene—Jean being a very well trained dog—and completed the scene admirably. Larry Trimble was paid for the use of Jean and a fee for himself. This is how he and Jean were 'discovered'."

From his research, Brown learned that after the death of Strongheart, Lawrence Trimble retired to his ranch in (he believes) San Gabriel, California. Years later, his father's grandmother, Jessie Ellen Brookes, Lawrence Trimble's aunt, moved across country in a dilapidated old truck from Maine to San Gabriel, where she permanently relocated. He speculates that the reason for her move was connected to Lawrence's permanent settlement in California.

Brown has some broadcasting experience, as does his nephew and his niece, Douglas Sanborn and Karen Sanborn. Doug has worked with Public Radio, and has also been employed with the making of documentaries. Karen has her Master's degree in communications and has worked in Maine radio and television studios.

"I think it is ironic how family genes/DNA really apply," Brown commented. "I am referring to my nephew and niece working in broadcasting, and that the majority of my family has a true love of dogs and enjoys training them. I have a Labrador retriever and Border Collie mix named Yankee Girl whom I take reenacting with me. I have trained her in a manner similar to a military working dog (not to attack) where she portrays a war dog or a mascot for Colonial, Civil War and WWII eras."[15]

Strongheart's influence on the motion picture industry, as well as his influence in studies in communication with non-human animal life, is substantial. J. Allen Boone, his caretaker, wrote *Kinship With All Life*, *The Language of Silence* and *Letters To Strongheart*. Boone was a direct descendant of Daniel Boone and had begun his wordsmith career as a journalist, then changed it to publicist for Robertson-Cole Pictures Corporation. He even produced *Kismet* for the company. He related in *Kinship With All Life* that his whole life was changed due to his encounters with the dog.

Strongheart showed him how an animal can nonverbally communicate with the human species, and vice versa. It all started with an incident with their sleeping arrangements, a mundane situation many pet owners have encountered. Boone had never owned a dog and had never kept one in his home. Since Strongheart was such a valuable movie star, Boone thought, he should sleep in the bed, not on the hard floor. The bed was placed against a wall. The first night was an ordeal with the former police dog getting up repeatedly to investigate noises, and each time settling back down with his derriere facing Boone in the bed, pushing him closer and closer to the wall each time. Needless to say, all this put the screenwriter in a bad humor in the morning. He told the dog that this was not going to happen anymore. Something different would have to be done!

Strongheart then tugged on his pajamas and brought him into a position to face the French windows of the bedroom. He took an end of one of the window

curtains in his teeth. Then he looked at Boone, then back at the curtains, and then back at Boone. A light went on in Boone's mind. The dog was trying to communicate that he needed to face the window each night to be ready in case of any danger from outside! A less observant man would simply have discounted the dog's behavior as the mindless meanderings of a dumb animal.

From that day on, the bed was turned with its head facing the windows so that Strongheart could feel more prepared and Boone could get a decent night's sleep. [16]

This was the beginning of a new focus for Boone's writing and research talents, and he is recognized today as an early expert in the field of nonverbal communication between species. He continued to learn from Strongheart and he went on to teach millions of others. *Kinship with All Life* and *Letters to Strongheart* have never been out of print since their publication dates over 54 years ago.

Strongheart's image helped sell canned dog food from 1931 to the early years of the 21st century. Many generations fed their dogs Strongheart dog food with the German Shepherd on the familiar blue and white label, and Strongheart cat food with the brown tabby kittens. Some pet owners probably never realized that the German Shepherd that emblazoned the dog food label represented a silent screen star. Doyle Packing Company of Kansas City, Missouri, Momence, Illinois, and Los Angeles, California, was the first company to sell Strongheart Dog Food. In recent decades, Allied Pet Foods of Atlanta, Georgia, sold this brand. The company merged with Simmons Foods of Siloam Springs, Arkansas in 2004 to become Simmons Allied Foods. The Strongheart label vanished from store shelves in 2003. Most recently, it was sold in K-Mart Stores.

CHAPTER TWO
HOLLYWOOD,
THE DOG HERO FACTORY

Hollywood is famous for borrowing ideas. Wolfheart, a dog with a name uncannily similar to Strongheart's, starred opposite Guinn ("Big Boy") Williams in the independent films *Courage of Wolfheart* (1925), *Fangs of Wolfheart* (1925), *The Big Stunt* (1925) and *Wolfheart's Revenge* (1925). Charles R. Seeling, who rented office space at Universal Studios, produced the Wolfheart series. Wolfheart was a sturdy, compact animal and in still photographs and surviving film he appears to have weighed about 70 pounds and resembled a Shepherd mix. *Wolfheart's Revenge* exists today and has all the elements of a typical action-filled dog hero film; thus, it merits attention. Guinn Williams plays "Smilin' Jack," a cattle ranch hand working for Richard Bronson (Captain Bingham).

He meets his boss' pretty flapper niece Betty (Kathleen Collins), and the two hit it off. The crooked foreman Blackie Blake (Larry Fischer) despises Jack because Betty prefers the younger man's attention. Even the gift of a paint horse fails to win him a kiss.

Blake, in a bid to win favor with his boss, volunteers to go over to the sheep rancher, "Williams" (an uncredited actor), and offer him a check from Bronson for half of his water. Williams declines, and Blake sees his opportunity to forge his signature on the check when Williams asks him to take a letter to the post at the

Don't Fail to See

Wolfheart

THE WONDER DOG

In his thrilling, diverting outdoor comedy-drama

"Fangs of Wolfheart"

— Added —

6th Chapter of
"SNOWED IN"
and COMEDY

edge of the main road. Blake secretly opens the letter. In it, Williams orders 500 lambs from a dealer, and adds that he does not plan to sell any water to the cattlemen. Blake copies his signature onto the check by holding it up to the light, then goes back to Williams and asks for the ingredients for a rolled cigarette. After he lights his cigarette, he puts the lighter (and the check) in Williams' shirt pocket. Blake then shoots him from a hidden location. Wolfheart sees Blake fleeing on horseback and gives chase. Williams' wife (Helen Walton) sees the dog chase the murderer, who is unfortunately too far away for her to identify. She is sure that the dog could identify her husband's killer. Blake complicates matters by framing Jack for cattle rustling and traps Wolfheart, tying him to a tree. He then kidnaps Betty, presumably to have his way with her. Mrs. Williams runs to Bronson for help when she encounters the ranch hands, who are about to hang Jack. Bronson for some reason, probably rooted in male chauvinism, dismisses her pleas until Wolfheart brings him the evil ranch foreman's coat. In its pocket, Mrs. Williams finds the letter her husband planned to mail the day he was murdered. Wolfheart then finds Jack. Jack commands him to help the villain, who, after a desperate fight with Jack, has fallen off a steep drop into a stream below. Wolfheart cannot keep the man's head above the current, so he saves himself. He then leads Jack to Betty, who has fallen off Blake's horse and is shaken but not badly hurt. Wolfheart is the glue that binds together the main characters. He introduces the lovers, and just by his existence, angers Blake, who hates anything having to do with Jack. Blake starts to beat poor Wolfheart for daring to bark at him when tied up to a tree. Jack punches him and Bronson breaks up the fight. Wolfheart saves his master's life when he brings Bronson Blake's coat, which holds the note written by the man he has

slain. Blake attempts to kill Jack and Wolfheart, but Jack still commands the dog to save the badman's life after he falls off a cliff into a stream. In a form of closure, the dog is unable to save the villain, and Jack and Betty can go on to a happy ending. In *Wolfheart's Revenge*, we have the archetypal elements of the majority of the dog hero films of the 1920s and 1930s: the dog, usually a male, is devoted to owner and master, also usually male, who is in his early 20s and who enjoys a healthy outdoor life and career. The owner may be an engineer for a large dam, a cowboy, a soldier returned from WWI, a prospector, a Mounted Police officer, or a civilian employee of the Forest Service. The plot generally revolves around the owner and a crooked—foreman or timber company or assessor or contractor. The owner's employer usually has a pretty daughter or niece staying at the facility for a month or two, and it is during this time that the main conflict occurs. The action usually is aggravated by theft, attempted abduction, sabotage, murder, animal cruelty or some combination of the above. The dog becomes a hero by using his canine instincts and intelligence to survive and be reunited with his owner who, with the help of a good woman stops the criminal—and the bad guys are always stopped—sometimes lawmen apprehend him, occasionally he is killed. Since he is cruel to both animals and humans, the audience is rarely sorry to see him go.

In some cases, the plot revolves around the dog instead of the human owner. The dog belongs to a handsome pioneer and his attractive family, who are surviving in the wilderness. Natural elements of the untrammeled area where they live are at once friend and enemy, celebrated and feared—ideas sharing the same stage as the plot progresses. The dog has to save the life of one of the family members when they are lost in the snow or trapped by rising flood-waters. Occasionally he has to rescue the miscreant of the film. Most of these films have one or more villains. Films lacking a villain, such as Rin-Tin-Tin's *A Hero of the Big Snows*, are more the exception than the rule.[1]

A third plotline, which developed early in the history of cinema, was the man rescues dog that later rescues man dynamic. This is seen in *Clash of the Wolves*, *Kelly and Me* and other 20th Century films. We see that tale reversed, in the 21st century production *Eight Below* (2006).

The 1920s truly was *the* decade for the heroic German Shepherd picture. Dog trainers were working on the sets of almost all the studios. FBO had Ranger; Warner Bros. had Rin-Tin-Tin, Paramount had Flash, United Artists and MGM had Peter the Great, First National and Associated Exhibitors and I.E. Chadwick had Strongheart, Chadwick and Sun Pictures Corporation had Lightnin', Universal had Dynamite, Charles R. Seeling Productions had Wolfheart, and Rayart had Lightning Girl. Napoleon worked over at Tiffany, Thunder worked at Fox, Lumas and Gotham, and Sandow labored at Chesterfield Motion Picture Corporation for the van Pelt brothers. Fearless was a German Shepherd who worked on a number of short films for Chesterfield, all of which are apparently lost.

Dogs were commonplace in films. However, the very large and the very small tended to be sought for comedies and the large working breeds like Siberian huskies, collies and German Shepherds dominated the genre. When the 1940s arrived and more and more dog films became aimed primarily at the juvenile moviegoer, in the film a child replaced the grown man and the suburbs and small towns edged out the high country of Montana or the desert of Nevada. However many dog heroes still performed their deeds in the great open spaces.

Few movie mutts are more completely forgotten than Peter the Great. Peter was a regal dog and a major studio star that began life as a shepherd dog in Prussia just after WWI ended. Life on the steppes was harsh and dogs usually died from disease if wolf packs did not kill them trying to get to the flocks. Peter's father had been a Red Cross dog in WWI; it was there that his owner, once an officer, Captain Adolphus von Heimreich, who was known as Fritz, had acquired the puppy Peter. The officer was decorated for his service, but after experiencing the horrors of war and knowing his family manufactured munitions to wage it, Fritz could no longer remain in the service. Nor did he have the desire to claim any of the family wealth. Renouncing the organized slaughter of his fellow man, he deserted the German Army and began a new life as a shepherd. An American discovered him working in the hills and asked if he could have Fritz's dog Peter for his son Edward, who would provide him with a comfortable life. Fritz agreed and the dog came to New York State. The new owner, Edward Faust, was convinced that this was the Red Cross dog who

SAM SAX
presents

PETER
THE
GREAT
The Miracle Dog of the Movies
in

THE SIGN
OF THE CLAW

ETHEL SHANNON

had helped him at the front when he served in the German Army, although his father thought that Peter was in fact the dog's sire, now buried by Fritz in the hills of Prussia.

Edward and his brother Arlis decided that this animal was intelligent enough and strong enough to have a career in motion pictures. The young men taught him jumping, landing, crawling, protecting, attacking, expressing emotions through barking and facial expressions, ladder climbing (a very difficult feat for any dog), and water tactics such as fetching objects and rescuing persons from the water. He also learned to find objects without lowering his nose to the ground and to disarm someone holding a wooden gun. This handsome German Shepherd got his start as a stunt double for Strongheart in *The Love Master* (1924), working on location at Banff National Park in Canada. Lawrence Trimble told the boys that their dog might get work as an extra or double for some films being made there, so they took a train to the Canadian Rockies. Strongheart refused to climb a mountain slope, and so Peter took on the job of stunt double. Producer Charles B. Dreyer met him and his owners, Arlis and Edward, and was most impressed with them. He became a co-owner of the dog soon after. According to his biographer, Clara M. Foglesong, Peter starred in the short films *Little Red Ridinghood* (1924) for Century Film Company and

Teasing Papa (1923), a Christie Comedy. Peter starred in the feature-length dramas *Sign of the Claw (1926)* and *King of the* Pack (1926) for Gotham Productions (Lumas Film Corporation), and was the star of *The Silent Accuser* for MGM. He shared billing with Edna Tichenor, later to become famous as the vampire girl in *London After Midnight* (1927). Peter had some famous costars in *The Silent Accuser*—Eleanor Boardman and Raymond McKee.[2] His master Jack is arrested and charged with murdering his grandfather. He is in prison awaiting trial. Peter risks his life to enter the prison, visits and makes friends with the warden, then goes out to find the real killer.

Frank O'Conner, assistant director of *The Silent Accuser*, said in an interview:

> By his ability to follow direction, [Peter] cut time and costs of
> production. The outstanding thing Peter could do was snarl.
> In fact, he was the only dog who could emote a snarl; that is,
> pretend anger when he was not angry....Peter could also crawl,
> something I could get no other dog to do. He would crawl as
> if escaping observation from somebody looking across the
> casement of a window. He would crawl along the floor, fol-

lowing a man whom he had known only a few days; a man in the play supposed to be escaping from prison. Peter would crawl in the same manner as the man in order to avoid detection from supposed prison guards who were watching him...he would bite the so-called villain of the play without marking him or doing injury. With other dogs, it was necessary to pad clothing—usually skin color—and to use gloves made of very tough leather.[3]

Peter impressed *The New York Times* film reviewer Mordaunt Hall:

Yesterday afternoon the audience on several occasions applauded Peter's feats, and there were sighs of regret when the dog was supposed to have been slain by a prison guard. Clapping signaled the pleasure of the people when they realized that crafty Peter had only been shamming death. The guard had lifted up the animal's hind legs, and as they fell limply to the ground, it was taken for granted that his end had come. But

Peter waited until all was still and then sprang free of the prison gate, eager to follow Jack in his escape from the jail….Peter may not be as good looking as Strongheart or Rin-Tin-Tin, as he is leaner. But he has a fine, black nose, intelligent, bright eyes, ears that are erect, alert to the slightest sounds, and legs that carry him with the speed and grace of a gazelle. [4]

Now a major Hollywood star, Peter's name was above those of his human costars in *Wild Justice*, a United Artists release of 1926.

The summer of 1926 was a bad season for film fans, for it was then that they lost both Rudolph Valentino and Peter the Great, both young stars whose careers would likely have gone on for years to come. Though he was as athletic and talented as Rin-Tin-Tin, Peter was not to go down in history as a canine superstar. One steamy evening, Peter was fatally shot when Edward Dreyer drove to the home of a friend by the name of Fred Cyriacks. Peter was in the backseat of the car. According to the Los Angeles Supreme Court trial, both men were intoxicated, and Cyriacks got into an argument over Peter, saying he did not like the dog because it had tried to bite him. He went into his house, got a rifle, and fired at Dreyer. Peter leapt up to defend his master and took the bullet in the neck.

The best veterinary care that money could buy failed to save the motion picture star. Dreyer sued twice. The Los Angeles Supreme Court on December 9, 1927 awarded the then-largest settlement for the death of a dog to its owner: $125,000.00. [5] In Dreyer v. Cyriacks 112 Cal.App. 279, 297 P. 35 (Cal.App. 1 Dist., Feb. 28, 1931), the court held that the trial court did not abuse its discretion in granting a new trial on the ground

A BLACK ALTAR

Peter the Great, the famous movie dog, was killed with a bullet poisoned with the same passion that destroyed the Carthaginian empire—envy.

He was a great dog. His rating in Dun and Bradstreet was $74,000, and that is more than many human beings are worth, in dollars at least. But Carthage was great, too, and the jealousy of Rome laid low her might.

"Carthage is greater than Rome," is the gist of the reason why Carthage was destroyed. "My dog is better than yours," is the reason why Peter the Great died on the altar of human envy.

Peter the Great's trainer got into an argument with a Los Angeles breeder of dogs. As the automobile bore Peter away, a rifle spat out the bullet that ended the great dog's life. Envy and its twin, jealousy, are the silliest and the costliest of ill-famed human desires.

that the verdict of $100,000 in compensatory damages and $25,000 in punitive damages was excessive. The court, however, made the following poetic rhetoric in its ruling:

> With reference to the question of the amount of the verdict, plaintiffs have cited us to an array of cases from 30 states of the Union and from England and Canada. But not one of them relates to the destruction of an animal. They all concern the death of or injury to human beings, and it is absurd to argue that in fixing damages the value of human lives and the value of dogs are to be measured by the same standard. As declared in section 491 of the Penal Code, "Dogs are personal property, and their value is to be ascertained in the same manner as the value of other property," but certainly the value of a human life is not to be so determined.
>
> Plaintiffs say in their brief: It must be remembered, that Peter the Great was a motion picture star, he was a gift to humanity. Peter the Great is a name that will go down in history as the most human like dog that ever displayed its skill in a film drama. His name was a symbol of loyalty, devotion, nobility, and heroic exploits. Peter the Great, king of the silver screen, was the playmate of mankind. He lived and struggled, suffered and sacrificed, to make countless thousands happy and cheerful. He made the multitude laugh and cry, wonder and admire. Peter the Great sent them to their homes with pictures of high ideals and unselfish service; the clean, the pure, the good in thought, example and action. Peter the Great was a by-word of every household, a wonderword to every child lover of the motion picture world. And when he came to the last scene, in the drama of life, when the curtain of death was slowly ringing down and he was going into that long, long sleep, I know he felt that it was only a new act he was performing as a part of his life work, as a part of some cruel tragedy, and he seemed to smile as the lights went out.

Whatever virtue there may be in the foregoing sentiments as a tribute to the memory of Peter the Great, they certainly carry little convincing force as a legal argument in support of the theory that the measure of damages for the destruction of a dog is or should be the same as the one applied in actions growing out of the death of a human being. (112 Cal.App. 279, 284-285.)

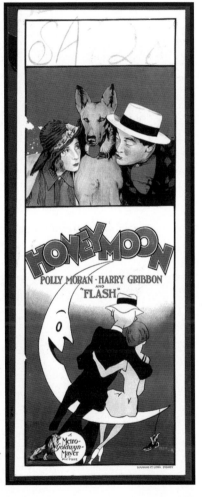

In 1945, Clara Foglesong published *Peter*, a sentimental and appealing, though not altogether accurate, account of the life and times of Peter the Great. It may be the only book covering the career of this dog, and is illustrated with rare stills from his films. Peter the Great's name has not lived on in the minds of movie lovers. With the exception of *The Sign of the Claw*, which became commercially available for purchase in February 2008 and is occasionally screened for the public in the Library of Congress' Mary Pickford Theater, his films appear to have not survived. The almost complete obscuration of the dog's films after the close of the silent era makes his death even more poignant.

Flash was a popular dog in the movies during the 1920s. He worked in a number of films like *Honeymoon* for Paramount and for MGM in *Shadows of the Night* (1928) and *Under the Black Eagle* (1928).[6] Flash was Paramount's only German Shepherd star of the 1920s. *Shadows of the Night* has apparently shared the same fate as *London After Midnight*—in other words, it is probably lost. *The Box Office Record* of 1929 published these reviews:

The dog of war finds his wounded master

A Grand Prairie, Texas theater owner remarked: "A well trained dog in a pretty fair picture. Underworld? Of course!" In another small town theater, the Paramount in Wyoming, Illinois, the proprietor praised the film with this comment: "Used this

"You know what happens when anyone tries to steal our women!"

one on my 10 cent bargain night and pleased very well." The LaCrosse, Kansas, theater manager had this to say about the film: "Better than the usual dog pictures. Had several comments on the cleverness and beauty of the dog, and just a few on the picture. Consequently, the dog must be the show."

"Positively no kidding, this dog is great!" enthused the manager of the Screenland Theatre located in Nevada, Ohio. "Draws for us and sends our patrons away singing praises. Good little picture, new print, lighter than usual for Metro. Of course, the story is no strain on an adult intellect and the cast is immaterial with such a dog. Lawrence Gray is the boy, Louise Lorraine is the girl. Warner Richmond makes a darn good chief villain, Molly Moran is something Ziegfield overlooked. [7]

Other canine movie stars included the clever Ranger. In the 1920s audiences would anxiously sit in lavish movie theaters as the lights dimmed and the electric curtain parted to reveal the latest Ranger picture. There he was, his barking, leaping image coming at the audience in startling black and white. His fangs flashing as he nabbed the bad guy, his bright black eyes gleaming with

The Dog Hero in Film

RANGER in "THE OUTLAW DOG"

love for his handsome young master—these became elements that kept the fans coming back time and again. The theater's piano or organ vibrated dramatically as Ranger opened his mouth. There were no barks heard in the theater; nevertheless, the barks were there, supplied by the audience's imaginations.

Ranger completed an incredible five pictures for FBO and Robertson-Cole Productions Corporation in 1928: *Fangs of the Wild, Dog Law, The Outlaw Dog, When a Dog Loves, Law of Fear, Dog Justice* and *Tracked*.[8] Of his nine films, only one, *Tracked*, is available on DVD. The DVD was made from a print

found in an old theater in Sweden in 2004. Hopefully, some movie theater or film archive has an intact copy of one of his other films and it will eventually come to light. *Tracked* (1928) in its extant form has a very short running time of only 48 minutes.

Sheep ranchers confront Jed Springer (Sam Nelson), a handsome newcomer in a remote community. They accuse his dog Ranger of killing sheep just because they find wool on his mouth. The wool comes from a lamb he has rescued, but no one saw the rescue except a little Husky dog. Ranger is framed by rancher Lem Hardy (Al Smith) because he knows his own dog is the sheep killer. Ranger is innocent; however, that does not stop Hardy

from knocking the dog unconscious, putting him in a burlap sack and throwing him off a cliff into a lake. Springer dives in after him and rescues him. "We both need to hide until I can prove you didn't do it," he tells the animal. He reasons that the sheep killings will continue and if everyone believes Ranger to be dead, they will see that he is not responsible for the killings. Meanwhile, he can track down the real killer.

Pretty Molly Butterfield (Caryl Lincoln) travels through the woods by wagon to visit her father, the richest guy in these parts. The driver is knocked out when the team turns too sharply and Molly can't reach the reins because they are dragging the ground. Ranger runs at breakneck speed alongside the wagon and takes the reins in his mouth, slowing the horses to a halt.

Nathan Butterfield (Clark Comstock) greets Lem Hardy, who comes to call on his daughter Molly. Hardy shows him an engagement ring meant for Molly. "Molly should see that she gets a gentleman for a husband."

Molly closes the box when Lem opens it to show her the diamond. "I'm sorry, Lem, I just simply don't love you." She then lets it slip to her father that a dog just saved her life, and his owner was so good to her. Hardy puts two and two together and cries, "That's Springer's dog! He tears sheep apart! I'll get him!"

Molly hurries to the woods and helps Springer and Ranger hide from a posse led by Hardy. Ranger gets loose briefly and is discovered by the ranchers hovering over a sheep corpse, licking it. They show this scene to Springer. Grief-stricken, he knows what he must do. Borrowing a horse, he gives chase to Ranger, who has fled back to the camp in the woods. Springer loads his pistol, and holds it above the cringing dog, reluctant to shoot. Meanwhile, Molly witnesses another killing of a sheep and shows the ranchers the real killer, Lem Hardy's dog. They kill the dog and then pursue Springer on horseback, hoping they can reach him before he executes poor Ranger. Molly is successful. In *Tracked*, Ranger, through no fault of his own, is accused of one bad deed after another. He is the very embodiment of the frustration felt by many of us who sometimes feel we cannot win for losing. Doing good deeds sometimes causes misunderstandings on the part of those we do the good deeds to benefit. Like Buster Keaton, Ranger in *Tracked* is the perennial put-upon character. He helps a lost sheep and everyone assumes he is a killer because he has a piece of wool on his mouth. At one point, ranchers attempt to kill him but his master intervenes just in time. The countryside is brimming over with dogs and the only one ever accused of anything seems to be poor old Ranger. The film has a plot echoing *The Night Cry* with Rin-Tin-Tin, albeit a slower paced one. Even so, this only known Ranger film serves as a valuable commodity to the film collector.

Ranger inspired a line of dog health products manufactured by the now-defunct Ranger Products Corporation of New Haven, Connecticut. The products included dog flea soap and worm medication, all with a handsome German Shepherd on the box. The flea powder and the flea soap could be had for 25 cents each.

Lightnin' the Police Dog was a star in many short films for Chadwick's "International Detective Series" and for Peerless Pictures Corporation. They included *Speed* (1926), *Blitz* (1926), *Honor* (1925), *Claws* (1925) and *Lightnin' Wins* (1926), which has been restored by the UCLA Film and Television Archives.[9]

Lightning Girl, "the screen's only white dog star," starred in *Call of the Klondike*, which is available on videocassette. This version, released in 1926, is not to be confused with the 1950 *Call of the Klondike*, which had no dog hero. The number of female canine actors of the American cinema is still quite small,

Paramount Theatre
☞ TODAY ☜

"Call of the Klondike"
With
Gaston Glass and Dorothy Dwan
A Good Comedy and Late News Reel

Wednesday and Thursday
Jack Perrin in "The Gray Devil"

but since 2000 some good ones have made a name for themselves in films like *Eight Below*. The reason for why there have not been many female dog actors (actresses) until very recently is undetermined.

Thunder shared marquee billing with none other than jazz-age superstar Clara Bow in *Black Lightning* in 1924. He also starred in *The Silent Pal* (1928). *Black Lightning* is a typical Gotham dog hero vehicle. War veteran Ray Chambers (Harold Austin) takes a vacation in the mountains while he recuperates from his wounds. With him is Thunder, a Red Cross dog who rescued him in France. Ray befriends Martha Larned (Clara Bow), who ekes out a marginal existence while supporting her younger brother, Dick (Joe Butterworth). As it turns out, Martha is the sister of Ray's deceased Army buddy Frank Larned (James P. Hogan). A local halfwit named Ez Howard (Eddie Phillips) bothers Martha almost daily. Ray stays with her to protect her from this rowdy and his brother Jim. Dick is injured one day and Ray leaves the cabin to seek medical help. Ez kills his own brother when he tries to rape Martha, then attempts to rape her himself. Thunder kills Ez, and Ray and Martha can look forward to a bright future.

Thunder is the real hero. If not for him, Martha would have met with the proverbial "fate worse than death," and the already depressed and war-shocked Ray would have lost all of his purpose in life.

In addition to *Black Lightning*, two other Thunder pictures still exist in private collections: *Wings of the Storm* (1926) and *Wolf Fangs* (1927).

For this book, Mr. Jere Guldin, film preservationist with the UCLA Film Vault, shared information about preserving *Black Lightning* and about film preservation in general.

Mr. Guldin graciously displayed several film vaults where the films donated to the UCLA are stored. Rows of film cans, stored upright in narrow rooms that are climate controlled, wait quietly like the treasures in a pharaoh's tomb. Some may be too deteriorated to be preserved using today's techniques. They must wait for better methods in the future. He illustrated this using a one-reel documentary from 1908. When the can was opened, a small cloud of red-brown powder emerged. The film's nitrate component had actually reacted with the inner surface of the can.[1] Mr. Guldin also opened a can containing a film of about the same age that had not yet deteriorated. Although it was made of nitrate cellulose, superficially it resembled any motion picture on safety film.

THUNDER THE MARVEL DOG

GOTHAM PRODUCTIONS

"HIS MASTER'S VOICE"

The University of California at Los Angeles has thousands of films stored in their vaults in Hollywood. The University pays the salaries of the film preservationists but the funding for the actual film preservation is from private donors. Big directors or big stars will help UCLA preserve the art of the past. Often writers and historians will finance a film's restoration. For example, David Stenn, author of the Clara Bow biography *Runnin' Wild*, paid for the restoration of *Black Lightning*. He tracked it down in Russia, where it was being stored in an old theater.

Jere Guldin works on silent films. Many of the prints he works with are the only known prints of the film in existence. The film preservationist needs to be guided by extra sources of material if there are missing scenes. These extra sources of material may include early versions of the script. After a film was first released, it may have been edited further. Music cues in the script help too. The script will contain the music cues, and titles as well. A specific title may be missing. Comparison of the titles with what the film preservationist already has will help fill in missing spots, as will production notes. It is a lot like detective work, especially when one considers that in the early days of filmmaking they did not make as many prints as they make of the modern films.

The Dog Hero in Film

Clara Bow, Thunder and Harold Austin in *Black Lightning*

If the film was color and the original has faded, how does the film preservationist restore the most accurate colors?

Mr. Guldin works mostly with black and white films but he has done a few color films. "If we have the nitrate," he advised, "we know what the original color was. The lab will match the colors." Tinting was done on many silent films to set the mood or the time of day.

Interestingly, Mr. Guldin observed, color was not at all uncommon in the original prints. In the time period of the infancy of film (1900 to 1930), it was the rare film that was in black and white. The 1930s brought an era of greater use of black and white film stock.

"*Black Lightning* was entirely amber toned except for the night scenes, which were tinted blue."

The major concern of anyone interested in preserving the treasures of the past is: how long will the restoration last? Should the preservation be in the form of a DVD?

Jere Guldin advised that the UCLA does not do much in the way of digital fixes. At this point, the end product is a print. This print is safeguarded and preserved. DVDs may be made for exhibition purposes only.

Clara Bow's films are a good example. She has a lot of appeal along silent film buffs. Some of her films have been released to video and to DVD. DVD is not the best archival method. In addition, one day the DVD will go out of favor and no one will be manufacturing the machinery to play the DVD.

"We have as of spring 2004 copied sections of *Black Lightning*," said Guldin, "and will preserve the whole film late this year (2004) or early in 2005." Thunder, the dog, has billing over Clara Bow as Martha Larned since it was released quite early in her career (1924) and before she became a star.

Mr. Guldin has restored another dog hero film of the 1920s, and shared his recollections. *Lightnin' Wins* (1926), a two-reel silent, starred a very young Gary Cooper. He remembered an amusing scene when Cooper tackled the villains of the picture and fumbled so badly that the dog and the female romantic interest had to save him.

John Hampton owned a silent movie theater in Hollywood once, and he closed up shop recently. He sold this, and the rest of his collection to a David Packard, who entrusted many of them to UCLA. I have also restored trailers for a film called *The Silent Flyer* (1926) starring a dog star I have not been able to identify.[2]

This trailer is part of the DVD boxed set, *More Treasures From American Film Archives: 50 Films, 1894-1931.* This massive collection of shorts and features was a collaborative effort between the Museum of Modern Art, the UCLA Film and Television Archive, the Academy of Motion Picture Arts and Sciences, the Library of Congress and the George Eastman House.

RIALTO

Today at 1—3—5—7—9

"Flash" The Wonder Dog in

THE

13TH HOUR

A Great Detective and Mystery Photoplay with
LIONEL BARRYMORE
Comedy - News - Organ

Mat. 10-20c.   Eve. 10-30c.

While some print reviews list Napoleon as the star of *The 13th Hour*, **other print ads list Flash the Wonder Dog as the star.**

Napoleon Bonaparte, a large German Shepherd, acted opposite a number of name stars like Mae Murray in *Peacock Alley* (1923) for Tiffany. That film is presumed lost. Lionel Barrymore costarred with Napoleon in *The 13th Hour* (1927) as a doctor with a split personality. The film is in a private collection and unavailable for viewing. Chester M. Franklin directed this film in which, in the words of Mordaunt Hall, *The New York Times* reviewer:

Napoleon

[I[t seems as though Lionel Barrymore had decided to invade Lon Chaney's thrilling realms. Here, Mr. Barrymore not only avails himself of an opportunity for disguises, but he also stresses the fact that one of his fingers is missing....Another contributor to the general excitement and fun in this subject is a police dog, known off the screen as Napoleon, and, in this production, as Rex...he is particularly eager to take a bite at

Professor Leroy (Mr. Barrymore), who gains no little satisfaction out of murdering people. The time he selects for his dark
affairs is one o'clock in the morning...Mr. Franklin has done
remarkably well with Napoleon, but here and there he permits
himself too much license. In one scene, Leroy has a wax
figure of himself seated at a desk and later he takes the place
of the dummy, the sleuths not being any the wiser. For once
Napoleon, who goes through nearly nine lives, does not make
the most of his acute sense of smell, which is, of course, Mr.
Franklin's fault.[10]

Klondike was a small, dark German Shepherd who worked in 1920s films.
In 1928, he acted in four pictures for Pathé, *Marlie the Killer, Fangs of Fate,*

 *Avenging Shadow* and *The
Law's Lash. The Law's Lash* is
the only known surviving Klondike film. George Pyper wrote
the screenplay and the director
was Noel Mason Smith, who
had directed *Clash of the Wolves*
(1925). Klondike stars as Scout,
a dog belonging to Mountie Ted

The above rare photo shows director Noel Mason Smith and his cast and crew on the set of *The Law's Lash*. (Photo courtesy Rae Malneritch and The Old Corral)

Campbell (Robert Ellis). Campbell hears rumors that a certain cabin in the forest is a hangout for fur smugglers. Campbell and several other Mounties astride their horses spend hours watching it from a distance. As they are outside the cabin, a lawman, Constable Maloney (Jack Marsh) is being murdered inside. Campbell and the other Mounties do nothing to prevent it and do not even pursue the fleeing killer. Campbell resigns to avoid being fired. His dog leaped through the window to help the Constable, and witnessed the dying man writing something on a flat piece of wood, a message that identified his killer, the local Factor, André La Rue (Richard R. Neil). Klondike is the only individual who knows where the piece of wood is because no one searches the cabin, and he brings it to the attention of Campbell's superiors. Campbell captures the smugglers and gets his position back. He then marries his girlfriend, Margery (Mary Mabery). Does Campbell really merit getting his position back after showing such apparent cowardice in initially failing in the basic requirements of his job? Just how forgiving are the Royal Canadian Mounted?

The camera operators display a reluctance to move close to their subjects, and the style of the acting and makeup appear more suited to those used in films made a decade previously. The villain (Neil) is costumed to resemble the sort of early film characters one would have seen in a Pearl White serial from 1919. He even has the trademark moustache, albeit without curling ends. Klondike is clearly the smartest character in the film. He brings the piece of wood to the attention of the Mounties, who missed it even though it was in plain sight.

Like any good dog, Klondike does not abandon his friend Campbell; in fact, one can almost sense sorrow in the dog's expression when he brings Campbell his red coat, as is his habit, and Campbell tells him he cannot wear it anymore. Klondike's faith in Campbell helps give the man the strength to find the killer. The dog gives the real Mountie the intestinal fortitude to do his job, and Klondike does not even get a salary.

Zimbo, a German Shepherd, was listed in the credits for *The Man Who Laughs*, a big-budget Universal costume drama released in 1928 as a silent with synchronized sound effects and a musical score. The film's main focus was on Gwynplaine (Conrad Veidt), even though the dog's heroics change everything in the closing half hour. Gwynplaine is a son of an English lord (also Conrad Veidt). who, during the late 1690s, insults King James II. The King's jester Barkiphedro (Brandon Hurst) gives Lord Clancharlie's young son to a Gypsy tribe who have a surgeon among their ranks. They use his skills to mutilate stolen children so they could be sold to fairs and traveling circuses. Lord Clancharlie

Conrad Veidt and Mary Philbin offer support to dog star Zimbo in *The Man Who Laughs*.

Homo (Zimbo) helps Dea the blind girl in *The Man Who Laughs*.

is killed in an iron maiden for offending the King. Young Gwynplaine, dumped by the Gypsies when they are banished from England for their crimes against children, makes his way to the wagon of Ursus (Cesare Gravina) who works in a traveling circus. The film then fast-forwards to a grownup Gwynplaine, who is struggling with his shame over his grotesque face and his love for a blind girl (Mary Philbin). Ursus keeps a big wolf (Homo) as companion and protector of Dea, the blind girl. Ursus would like to see the two marry. Gwynplaine is convinced that he is unworthy of her love. The insolent Countess Josiana (Olga Baclanova) attends one of their primitive plays, which culminates with Gwynplaine showing his grotesque eternal grin. She gives Gwynplaine a note promising an evening of bliss. Gwynplaine cannot turn her down. "She has seen my face and still would love me?" He decides that if she could love him, perhaps he will be worthy of Dea's love. Josiana is interested merely in the novelty of the experience.

The Dog Hero in Film

Thanks to the bravery of Homo, Dea and Gwynplaine are reunited in *The Man Who Laughs.*

Josiana receives Gwynplaine with enthusiasm and then receives a letter from the Queen informing her that to keep her fortune she must marry a descendant of Lord Clancharlie, and Gwynplaine is that descendant. She laughs at the notion and Gwynplaine departs, to return to Dea. Soon after, the scheming Barkiphedro, trying to get rid of all evidence that Gwynplaine is a Peer, has him arrested and thrown in prison. Queen Anne (Josephine Crowell) discovers his plans and gets "the laughing man" out of prison. The Queen presents Gwynplaine to the House of Lords. Homo attempts to lead Dea to the gates of the palace where Gwynplaine is being presented, and is driven off by guards. His barking alerts Gwynplaine to their presence. He learns that Dea and Ursus have been told that he was executed. The heartbroken pair have booked passage out of town on a sailing ship, planning to take their wolf with them. Barkiphedro tries to stop Gwynplaine from reaching the ship on time. Homo waits in a small boat waiting to load passengers onto the ship. The wolf sees Barkiphedro escaping Gwynplaine and murdering members of a mob, which has risen up to defend "the laughing man." The cruel former jester attacks the young man at the docks as he tries to reach the boat. Homo leaps into action and tears out Barkiphedro's throat so that Gwynplaine can reach the boat and start a new life with his three friends. The dog is present as an important character throughout the picture. He functions as a gentle guide for Dea as well as a guard dog. He attempts to reunite Dea and Gwynplaine on two attempts and is finally successful; thus, he is the link that holds this interesting family unit together. Homo's ferocity, entirely necessary in the final scene, makes for a satisfying ending.

It is appropriate that Germany should have a German Shepherd cinematic dog hero also. Germany's silent dog star, Grief, starred in *Sein Bester Freund* (1929) with young

German's silent dog German Shepherd Grief and best friend Harry Piel in *Sein Bester Freund.*

actor/director Harry Piel. The film and its remake are lost. A young Alfred Hitchcock, then working exclusively in his homeland of Great Britain, featured a German Shepherd dog hero in his thriller *The Mountain Eagle* in 1926. This film, too, is apparently lost.[11]

Some information about the plot can be reconstructed from contemporary film reviews. A retailer in a Kentucky town wants to marry a local teacher who is not interested in him. The shopkeeper takes revenge and accuses her of molesting his mentally ill son. The teacher marries a local hermit to try to restore her standing in the community. The two genuinely fall in love and have a son. Pettigrew, still not satisfied, then hides his own son and accuses Fulton of murdering him. What follows is an exciting and suspenseful hunt for the Fulton family, who

An unknown dog in the lost film *The Mountain Eagle*

have fled to the mountains.[12] We can assume the involvement of a dog hero by the publicity stills and lobby cards that were created for the film's release.

CHAPTER THREE

THE ANIMAL THAT SAVED WARNER BROS.

Rin-Tin-Tin had his origins during WWI. An American infantryman, Lee Duncan, found two frightened and starving German Shepherd puppies in a hastily abandoned German kennel on the front lines in Fluiry, France. There was nothing that the tall blond youth could do for the German Shepherd message dogs in the outside kennels. All lay dead, killed in a bombing. However, he heard whimperings and found a female and very young puppies in a burrow. The mother had saved herself and the puppies by tunneling underground to have her litter. The men adopted her and the puppies. Lee took two and named them Nanette and Rin-Tin-Tin after little cotton batting good luck dolls that French girls sold the troops. Duncan kept both puppies with him and was able to ship them to the States after his duty ended. Both pups contracted distemper and despite medical treatment, Nanette died. When Duncan reached the States, he purchased another female German Shepherd as a companion to the male puppy and named her after Nanette.

Duncan returned to his civilian job at a hardware store in the Los Angeles area and began entering the now recovered Rin-Tin-Tin in high jump competitions. He decided to enter the realm of motion pictures because of the success of Strongheart. He knew he had a clever dog—Rin-Tin-Tin was devoted and answered only to him. For his first job, the dog starred in a silent short, *My Dad* (1922), for Film Booking Offices of America (FBO). After training the dog for many months, Duncan went to Warner Bros. studios when he saw an ad in a trade paper for a wolf dog to act in *Where the North Begins* (1923). He groomed the dog thoroughly, only to find that the part required him to look like a scruffy wild animal.[1] The stunts the dog was asked to do in this picture involved an amazing high jump. After his starring role, "Rin," as his owner called him, went on tour to promote the picture.

Rin-Tin-Tin was a versatile pooch that could climb a flight of steps, open doors and pull knobs using his mouth, act contrite, and even jump out of a pit. Granted, doubles handled some stunts that the dog star did not do well, but Rin-Tin-Tin had done all of them himself at one time or another in his career.

"WHERE THE NORTH BEGINS"

FEATURING
RIN~TIN~TIN, THE FAMOUS POLICE DOG

DIRECTED BY
CHESTER M·FRANKLIN
A HARRY RAPF PRODUCTION
ADAPTED FOR THE SCREEN BY
FRED MYTON AND CHESTER M·FRANKLIN

WARNER BROS
Classic of the Screen

THE OTIS
LITHOGRAPH CO.

STYLE A

Where the North Begins was written by Raymond L. Schrock and Lee Duncan and edited by Lewis Milestone, who went on to become one of the premiere directors in Hollywood. Some of his credits include, and the films

Of Mice and Men (1939), *Ocean's Eleven* (1960) and the television series *Have Gun, Will Travel* (1957-1963). Rin-Tin-Tin's big-budget debut told the story of a German Shepherd pup that falls out of a crate being shipped across the Canadian countryside via dogsled. Wolves adopt and raise him. The film moves its focus to the life of a French-Canadian named Gabrielle Dupré (Walter McGrail). Dupré attempts to make a fur run to Skagway, Alaska, for the local factor, Shad Galloway (Pat Hardigan). Instead, he loses his team and sled after being shot in the arm by an unknown assassin. The Wolf Dog sees the man lying in the entrance to a cave and considers eating him, but the human/dog bond forged over thousands of years stops him. He also drives off members of his own pack when they get too close. The assassin (Charles Stevens), known as The Fox, comes to finish the job he started. The Wolf Dog attacks him and tears off a piece of his clothing. Dupré finds shelter in a cabin built for the use of couriers like him. He knows that he has to carefully guard that piece of fabric ripped from his would-be assassin and keep it out of reach of his canine companion. "You know who this belongs to, and you find him for me!" he reminds The Wolf Dog.

The assassin works for Galloway, who wants to eliminate Dupré so he can romance his pretty girlfriend, Felice McTavish (Claire Adams). He has a mistress of his own, but that does not stop him from desiring Felice. Galloway had retrieved the dogs and the furs and sold most of them. Dupré surprises Galloway by showing up at his office with The Wolf Dog. The Wolf Dog lunges at The Fox and a Mountie fails to notice that the piece of fabric the courier has is the same color and type as the fabric of The Fox's clothing. Galloway was sure he had gotten rid of the trapper. No matter; there are still other ways to rid himself of the competition. He accuses Dupré of lying about being ambushed so that he can divert the Mounted Police's suspicion away from himself. He tells The Fox to plant furs in the French-Canadian's cabin.

Meanwhile, a problem develops when The Wolf Dog appears to be jealous of an orphaned baby Dupré is tending, and the poor pup is banished to the outside.

A day later, the dog hears a scuffle in Dupré's cabin and helps a Native American caregiver protect Dupré's adopted son from The Fox. The only way in is through a second story window, 10 feet off the ground, and we see the our hero twice make a running start to gain a foothold on the sill. Dupré almost shoots The Wolf Dog when he erroneously jumps to a wrong conclusion about the dog after finding blood all over the floor of his cabin, and the baby and governess have gone missing!

Felice comes to the cabin just in time to prevent Dupré from putting a bullet to his own loyal friend's head. She explains that the baby and his caretaker are at her cabin. The Wolf Dog leaves the scene to try to tear The Fox's arm off before the villain confesses his and Galloway's crimes to the Mounted Police. Hurt by the betrayal of his human

An ALL TALKING SERIAL IN TWELVE THRILLING CHAPTERS

Nat Levine presents

RIN-TIN-TIN

In the greatest of all serials

Hear the tum tums of the Indian tribes

See the Indian attack

See the capture of the wolf-man.

DO YOU LIKE ACTION AND HAIR RAISING THRILLS!

You will see Indians attacking the whites—Indian warfare in all its horrors—action—fights and romance and the most thrilling suspense you have ever witnessed.

Enough adventure to last you for a lifetime—be sure and not miss the First Episode!

friend, the stray turns and heads into the forest. Meanwhile, Galloway makes a daring break while being led to the town lockup. Stealing one of the Mounties' horses, he takes off in a mad dash, pausing only to abduct Felice as she searches the woods for The Wolf Dog. This gives Rin-Tin-Tin the actor a chance to show off more stunt abilities as he leaps off a bluff to grab the villain. Galloway falls off a cliff while struggling with the animal. The Wolf Dog, unharmed, returns to the tall pines, and a cheerful closing shot finds him returning to the Dupré cabin months later with his own mate and litter of pups in tow.

The scene where Dupré blames the The Wolf Dog when he finds blood splattered in the cabin and the baby missing is familiar to students of European myth and folklore. Llewellyn, a prince of 12th-century Wales, is said to have come home one day to find his baby, Owain, missing from his crib, blood near the crib, and his dog Gelert alone in the house. Assuming the dog killed and ate the child, Llewellyn ran his sword through the dog, only to find the body of a wolf (some narratives identify the animal as a snake) in another room and the baby unharmed. The faithful hound had saved the baby.[2] Fortunately this cinematic re-enactment does not end the same way, as the real miscreant is brought to justice.

The Wolf Dog spends much of his time in *Where the North Begins* trying to get the villain and being ignored by inept authority figures. Finally, our stalwart hound chases The Fox to the steps of the Mounted Police headquarters where he is finally apprehended. Dupré is ambivalent toward his friend, who saved his life twice, once from wolves and once from The Fox. Dupré wants to love The Wolf Dog, but has spent so much time in the wild that he is distrustful. It is after The Wolf Dog runs away from him that he realizes just how much he cares for the dog. When The Wolf Dog returns with a mate and a litter of puppies, the family unit is intact.

Warner Bros. had a bad year in 1922 and was on the verge of bankruptcy, but *Where the North Begins* was such a success that Lee Duncan and his dog were guaranteed a long-term contract. Rin's second film for Warner Bros. was *Find Your Man* (1924). Darryl Zanuck, then 22, wrote the script for this melodrama about a dog whose master (handsome Eric St. Clair) is accused of murder. The dog was the only witness that can clear his master's name.[3] The film made a fortune, but is unfortunately another lost piece of cinema history.

Clash of the Wolves (1925) has moments of comedy but is mostly a straightforward drama. A

Dave (Charles Farrell) sends Lobo (Rin-Tin-Tin) for help in *Clash of the Wolves*.

mountain wolf pack migrates to the Mojave Desert after a fire destroys their habitat. Rin-Tin-Tin plays Lobo, the half dog and half wolf leader of the pack. Nanette, his real life mate, portrays his wild mate in the film and a litter of German Shepherd pups imitate wolf cubs. The pack of wolves is stock footage of real wolves, which was spliced in with footage of German Shepherd dogs. The pack singles out a cow from a herd, forcing ranchers go after them on horseback. Lobo heroically leads a group of ranchers away from his pack but is badly hurt when he falls on a yucca. A young borax prospector, Dave Weston (Charles Farrell), finds Lobo wandering the desert. Lobo has left his pack to die alone. Dave knows he could make some money off a reward for Lobo, but the young man's compassion triumphs. He removes a yucca thorn from Lobo's paw, and applies disinfectants and bandages. The wolf dog becomes his loyal ally. Weston announces to his girlfriend, May Barstowe (June Marlowe), that he has just discovered a borax deposit that will bring him substantial wealth. He and May visit Horton, the local chemist, to have a sample appraised. Horton (Pat Hartigan) instructs his assistant to lie and say he is out of testing fluid and that it will be several weeks before the results are in. This tactic will buy him time to find out the location of the mine. Dave files a claim as he awaits word from Horton.

May's father does not approve of her relationship with Weston. An amusing scene has one of his hands (comic relief Heine Conklin as Borax Bill) instructed to keep an eye on them as they sit in the drawing room, ostensibly identifying mineral specimens. Borax Bill notices that Lobo, disguised as a bearded dog (an Old English sheepdog, perhaps?), uses his thumping tail to warn the lovers when anyone approaches. "If I come back and find them making love, you're fired!" Barstowe tells Bill. He then leaves to fix some fences damaged in a sandstorm. Bill takes off his shoes and tries to drive Lobo away with his smelly socks. Lobo simply turns around. Bill then tempts Lobo with a kitten. Lobo ignores him. Running out of ideas, Bill tells May that he is going to tell on them! May promises him a kiss if he keeps mum. She gives him a peck on the cheek. He is not satisfied. "I want a kiss like Dave gets," says Bill. Barstowe the elder returns from fence repairs just as May gives Bill a big smooch on the lips. Her father fires the hired hand on the spot.

Dave leaves in the middle of the sandstorm because he is suspicious of Horton and wants to erect a sign at his claim, but Horton follows him, then ambushes and shoots him, leaving him to die alone. Horton is attacked by Lobo and throws the dog over his shoulder in a body slam, escaping as the dog whimpers in pain. Weston's loyal wild friend has not deserted him, and drags the man to a cave. Using charcoal, Dave writes a message on his canteen for May: "May—Am Injured—follow Lobo—Dave," and hangs the canteen around Lobo's neck. Lobo goes to town and sees Horton with May. His desire to seek vengeance distracts him temporarily and he leaps on the cold-blooded killer. Escaping Lobo's jaws, Horton calls out to townspeople that the hated wolf is in their town. Lobo must flee to safety. In a tense scene typical of Warner Bros.' Rin-Tin-Tin features, May holds the canteen in her hands and does not see the message which is facing away from her, but Horton and his accomplice do see it. Lobo runs to May's ranch, eludes her pistol-toting father (Will Walling), and finally brings the girl to Weston's side. Horton finds them, kicks Dave while he lies bleeding, and forces May onto his horse, riding off along a desert road. Lobo, watching, has his own strategy. Howling, he summons his pack and they pursue Horton, who drops May to save himself. He falls off his horse, and is torn to pieces by the wolf pack. The film concludes with another scene involving puppies.

Rin-Tin-Tin's Lobo is another noble beast that could use some human love. He is hurt when engaged in the altruistic act of leading the posse away from his pack and his injury to disappear and die alone rather than have the pack turn on him, as they sometimes do to a wounded comrade. While Lobo brings out the best in Dave, he brings out the worst in May's father. Horton is irredeemable anyway, and would be cruel whether the dog were present or absent. In September 2004, this film was restored by the Library of Congress and made available for purchase through Image Entertainment as part of the DVD collection *More Treasures From American Film Archives: 50 Films, 1894-1931.*

Picture Play Magazine reviewed the film in its February 1926 issue:

> *The Clash of the Wolves* shows that incomparable canine, Rin-Tin-Tin, surrounded by his usual quota of bad actors. He is again a wolf tamed by a man's kindness, and shot at but never hit by a lot of old meanies. I have never seen him so good as he is in this picture. In one scene, he wears little boots and unlaces them himself, and at all times, he displays startling intelligence. Like Jackie Coogan, he is an actor who is worthy of better material and better support.

The Night Cry (1926) was another canine hit. Rin plays a sheep dog accused by sheep ranchers of killing their lambs. It does not help matters that whenever lamb carcasses are found partially eaten, his whereabouts are always undetermined. The real killer is a California condor. Rinty gets into a fight with a sheepherder's collie and everyone assumes that the collie is defending its

flock. Rinty's owner, John Martin (John Harron), promises his compatriots that he will slaughter the dog. He takes the dog home with him and tells his wife of the supposed misdeeds. John cannot bring himself to kill the dog, and he and his wife (June Marlowe) hide the animal in the cellar. An especially vindictive and distrustful sheepherder, Miguel Hernandez (Gayne Whitman), comes to the house looking for Rinty. He even tries to get their toddler daughter (Mary Louise Miller) to disclose the location of the dog. Later, when the husband is not at home, Hernandez makes another surprise visit and sees the end of a rope, which leads to a closed cellar door set in the wooden floor. Hernandez sees the rope move and opens the door. Mrs. Martin attacks him to save the dog, and kicks the gun into the cellar. Hernandez pushes her into a closet and puts a wooden rod through the latch. He then reaches for his gun and Rinty attacks him. Hernandez hits his head on the corner of the fireplace and is knocked unconscious. The crying baby wanders out of the cabin door as her mother struggles to push up the small rod to escape and go to her child.

Meanwhile, the other sheep ranchers have seen the condor killing a sheep. "So that's the real killer," one of them remarks to John. "Too bad you shot Rinty."

"But I didn't. He is safe at the house."

Unfortunately, the dog is far from safe, as he is still tethered to the rope in the cellar, and his potential executioner is still in the house. He barks furiously at the condor, which has spied the baby outside. It decides she might make a tasty meal if it can carry her to its cliff top nest. The mother finally escapes just as the bird bears that baby aloft. She and the dog follow the bird over the rocks and Rinty battles it to the death. As Rinty, Rin-Tin-Tin is the meat and potatoes of the film, providing most of the suspense and pathos.

Herman C. Raymaker masterfully directs the film, especially the nail-biting scenes in which the family hides the dog from the sheepherder and Hernandez reacts to a noise in the bedroom as he sits in the Martin kitchen. The Martins look at each other helplessly. Hernandez rushes to the room and sees what looks like a dog's tail under a bed. He pulls it out and finds that it is a fur rug. He leaves as the family breathes a sigh of relief. But where is Rinty? He hops out from under blankets in the baby's cradle. Rin-Tin-Tin must have understood something about what his job entailed, because he displayed the kind of emotion toward these actors that would be a spontaneous and genuine show of affection when observed in a non-acting dog. The scene in which he looks back and forth between Mr. Martin and Mrs. Martin as they glare scoldingly at him in the cabin shows that the film needed no soundtrack or schmaltzy theme song in the background to evoke laughter and sympathy.

Picture Play Magazine praised the film in its July 1926 issue:

> *The Night Cry*, with that incomparable actor, Rin-Tin-Tin, is another not-so-good story, depending on its leading character. Rin-Tin-Tin is more amazing than ever. I shouldn't be a bit surprised to hear that he was to try 'Dr. Jekyll and Mr. Hyde'…In New York, Rin-Tin-Tin made personal appearances with this picture, and if he comes to your town, by all means go to see this scholar and gentleman. Go, even if he tries to sell you a complexion cream after the performance. (No, he doesn't really.)

The film unfortunately reinforced a misperception in 1926 that this largest of the vultures is a predator when in fact it is exclusively a scavenger of carcasses.

Its ungainly naked-looking head and huge black body make the California condor seem sinister, and most filmgoers of that time probably never questioned whether it was in fact a dangerous bird to sheep or children. It was becoming quite rare even in 1926 and few audience members had ever seen one. Some state laws forbade the shooting of or the gathering of eggs of non-game birds like the condor. Such laws were sporadically enforced. The California condor population decreased even further until the species became so endangered that the remaining living wild birds were rounded up by 1987 and enrolled in a captive breeding program. The U.S. Fish and Wildlife Service released most of them into their native habitats. The Fish and Wildlife Service must authorize any use of condors or their captive breeding.[4]

Bozo, the individual condor actor in *The Night Cry*, was the only California condor in captivity at that time. Careful viewing of the film reveals that a stuffed feather bag was its double in the long shots where Rin-Tin-Tin kills it. Interestingly, Baby Louise Miller shares several scenes with the bird and shows no fear of it. In South America, semi-tame Andean condors once wandered town streets to keep them free of small animal carcasses in the days before they, too, became an endangered species.

The Night Cry addresses the perceived value of animals in an early 20th-century United States agrarian community. The truly valuable animals in the eyes of the sheepherders are sheep, and their value is a function of how much each animal can fetch on the market. Every other animal serves a subservient function relative to livestock. The dogs exist to protect the sheep and all predators are threats to the sheep; thus, they must be exterminated forthwith. If a dog begins to prey, it too must be immediately exterminated. It will not be given to someone who would take it to a city to be a pet or to work as a guard dog for a factory. The filmmakers challenge this notion and show that each animal is an individual deserving of fair treatment and a fair evaluation if accused of some misdeed. Rinty's story is a moral tale advising caution on the part of humans when rushing to judgment.

Warner Bros. arranged for 18 dogs to be trained to double for Rin over the course of his career with the studio. Thus, one has to watch closely in the action scenes to be sure that it really *is* Rin-Tin-Tin in those shots. In the 1926 *While London Sleeps*, Howard Bretherton, rather than Chester Franklin, directed Rin-Tin-Tin. The furred wonder teamed up with Scotland Yard vs. a master criminal named The Hawk and his ape-man.[5] The creature was George Kotsonaros, who played a similar role in *The Wizard* at Fox the following year. Unfortunately, this horror/mystery is lost.

Tracked By The Police (1927) opens with a close-up of Rin-Tin-Tin as the noble German Shepherd Satan. The titles describe him as "Loyal, true, with the heart of a lion and the soul of a child." By now, the dog was a star and Warner Bros. never missed an opportunity to open his pictures with a pose on some rocky crag as the heroic star majestically surveys the scenery below.

Jason Robards, Sr., is Bob Owen, a young engineer/inspector supervising the contractors for a dam project near the Arizona/California border. His constant companion is Satan, who had saved his life when a Red Cross dog on the front during WWI. Bob's boss, Tom Bradley (Wilfrid North) is injured on the job and his daughter Marcella (Virginia Brown Faire) comes to the project site to take care of him. To make things worse, the contractor, Sandy Sturgeon (Tom Santschi), has been taking bribe money from a rival firm to sabotage the new lower dam before it is even completed. Sturgeon tells his partner in crime, Wyoming Willie (Dave Morris) to poison Satan, turn the crew against Owen and then open the floodgates on the upper dam. Not content to limit his evil to destroying the project and flooding the valley, Sturgeon also attempts to kill the young engineer. Bob falls down a mineshaft and Satan finds him. He attaches a note to his collar to give to Marcella back at the office. Satan walks

across the crest of the dam to reach her, and is shot and injured in the paw by one of Sturgeon's henchmen minutes before he delivers the note. She reads it just as the villain arrives to molest her. In a highly suspenseful scene, Marcella, knowing that the nasty Sturgeon will kill the dog if he sees him, hides Satan in a grandfather clock. Sturgeon and his henchmen use Nanette, Marcella's dog, to track down Satan. The trusting dog leads them straight to the office. "We know that you're hiding that devil dog here!" Sturgeon shouts. Marcella insists that Satan is not there. Nanette's nose takes her to the grandfather clock. Sturgeon shoots the clock, opens it, and finds that there is no dog inside. Marcella breathes a sigh of relief. Just when Marcella believes that the dog is safe, Sturgeon feels small drops of blood falling on his hand. He looks up to see a tiny chink in the ceiling and realizes that the animal is in the attic. He hurries there with the intent of shooting Satan. Sturgeon's gun jams and the dog leaps out of a window and escapes.

Sturgeon then seizes Marcella. She grabs pepper from the kitchen table to throw at his face, but he seizes it and flings it into her eyes, blinding her. He then commands his men to take Nanette down to the river to drown her, as she is of no further use to him. They all leave when they learn that Bob Owen has escaped and is going out to notify the authorities. They open the floodgates a second time. The climax occurs when Marcella leaves the office, half-blinded by the pepper, to find the floodgates and close them. A crane boom snags her blouse and swings her out over the raging waters. Satan sees her peril and also that the villains have tied up Nanette with chains and have thrown her into a shallow tributary. He has to make a choice to save the girl or save the mate. He saves the girl, and then goes to save the mate, who has somehow escaped her bonds and reached shore. Bob finds Marcella and the dogs and we know that the heroine's blindness is only temporary; she will see again.

The Satan character manages to save the day in more fanciful ways than usual in a film of this type, a rescue more likely found in an action-packed serial. The dog knows that certain levers at the dam plant will open and close the floodgates, and he moves them with his jaws. He also has to make a split second decision about who to rescue—Nanette or Marcella? He pulls the young woman in before she falls into the floodwaters and then goes to find the dog. From the very beginning Sturgeon sees Satan and Bob as a threat to his scheme. The dog's presence seems to provoke the villain into greater violence against Bob than is necessary to sabotage the dam. Thus, the dog serves as a fulcrum for the dramatic elements of the story.

The scene where Satan walks across the dam crest is real. The film crew pushed its luck with this scene, but the luck of Rin and Warner Bros. almost ran out in 1928. The year 1928 was a banner year for Rin. He starred in *A Race For Life, Land of the Silver Fox, Million Dollar Collar* and *Rinty of the Desert*. During the filming of the latter film at a real dam, the Laguna Dam over the Colorado River, Rinty began the same crest-walking stunt that he did without injury in *Tracked by the Police*. However, this time, he lost his footing and clung precariously to the edge of the crest. Duncan got down on his knees and closed his eyes, sure that his dog would fall to his death in the waters below. Rin-Tin-Tin's physical strength saved him; he pulled himself up

and walked across to safety. Modern filmgoers might well wonder if Lee Duncan spent some sleepless nights over the course of Rin-Tin-Tin's career pondering whether his canine star's next picture would be his last. The American Humane Association had not yet come into existence. The AHA will not permit such a shot; scenes involving great heights or torrents of water now have to take place inside a studio.

D. Ross Lederman, who directed Rin in two pictures, commented once on the amazing relationship the dog had with Duncan. The dog could recognize chalk marks on the floor in lines and circles and understood that this meant the path and the movements he was to take. Often, only one rehearsal was needed, and the dog knew his course.

Tiger Rose (1929) was an early talking picture for Rin, who played Scotty, companion to a Native American woman named Tiger Rose (Lupe Velez).[6] The film survives in the collection of the University of Wisconsin at Madison.

Warner Bros. had a knack for finding screenwriters who could craft ac-

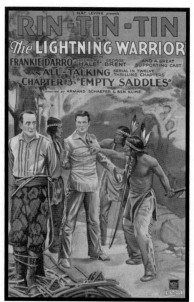

tion-packed stories for Rin and sympathetic characters for his compatriots. The films were not saccharine, and even if the dog hero sometimes displayed intelligence that a dog really does not possess, the pacing and dramatic situations made up for this weakness.

Warner Bros. executives decided that the dog was too old by 1930 to work in more pictures. Rather than give the dog a hard-earned pension and a lavish retirement party that would have been a boon for public relations, they unceremoniously let him and Duncan go. Duncan and his dog began working for Nat Levine and Mascot, doing

the serials *The Lone Defender* (1930) and *The Lightning Warrior* (1931). Rin was definitely old now and his famous features were seen only in close-ups, since other dogs were handling the stunts. Rin-Tin-Tin died in 1932 of natural causes at the age of 14 in the arms of Jean Harlow, who lived across the street from him and who saw the dog collapse in his front yard.

Lee Duncan buried Rin's body in the soil of his native France.[7] He has a star on the Hollywood Walk of Fame at 1623 Vine Street. In modern times, the public often confuses him with his great grandson who acted in a Screen Gems television production of the 1950s. Of Rin-Tin-Tin films, only *The Lightning Warrior, Where the North Begins, The Night Cry, The Show of Shows, Tracked By The Police, Tiger Rose, The Lone Defender, The Lighthouse By The Sea, The Hills Of Kentucky* and *Clash of the Wolves* appear to exist. Very little information exists about Nanette today. The

two had several offspring. Rinette was trained for a career in pictures, and two male puppies were also prepared for films, but only one, Rin-Tin-Tin, Jr., had any significant career. He acted in many films for Mascot Pictures, including *Law of the Wild*, *Vengeance of Rannah*, *Skull and Crown*, *The Test*, *Pride of the Legion*, *Wolf Dog* and *The Adventures of Rex and Rinty*. All of the above films have survived with the exception of *Pride of the Legion*. In *Law of the Wild* and *The Adventures of Rex and Rinty*, he shared the marquee with Rex the Wonder Horse, a black Morgan who had an impressive resume in motion pictures, not in spite of his innate wildness, but because of it.

Vengeance of Rannah (1936) is a typical Rin-Tin-Tin, Jr. Western. James Oliver Curwood wrote the original story. Pop Warner and his dog Rannah (Rin-Tin-Tin, Jr.) are taking the Cloverdale Bank's armored car to a large city. En route, Warner is shot and the car crashes. Rannah survives but the killers escape with the cash. Warner's daughter Mary (Victoria Vinton) maintains that her father is innocent of embezzlement. Local banker Frank Norcross (Roger Williams) is especially set on making him look guilty.

Some time later, insurance investigator Ted Sanders (Bob Custer) arrives. He finds Warner's body in a gully, guarded by his growling dog. Ted makes friends with Rannah and takes him back to town. Someone tries to shoot the loyal hound through the window of the bank while Ted discusses his findings with Norcross. Ted decides that Rannah is in danger because he can identify the killer. He leaves the dog at Mary's ranch. A man (Ed Cassidy) identifying himself as Deputy Sheriff Barlow prowls outside the ranch house and Ted confronts him. They agree to team up to solve the case. Mary, alone with Rannah, hears a knock at the door, assumes it is Ted, and opens it to find two men who are there to kill the dog. Rannah gets away and finds Ted. Barlow has tied him up and left—pretty odd behavior for a deputy sheriff. After the insurance investigator finds an older man (Wally West) who has been shot and left for dead in a barn, he puts two and two together. Rannah behaves aggressively toward the man. Ted deduces that the criminal exchanged his clothes with the local deputy sheriff. The dog is responding to the bad man's smell on the clothing. Doctor Adams (John Elliott) treats Barlow and Ted decides to bait a trap. The doctor conducts an inquest for the "dead" deputy. The

fake deputy shows up as part of his impersonation. Norcross also attends. Ted proves that Norcross staged the robbery of the armored car and hired the false deputy to cover his tracks.

A mistake in the film occurs in the scene with the inquest. Earlier in the film, Ted maintains that Rannah will bark and growl every time he encounters his master's murderer, and thus the killers may be gunning for him. However, the dog is present during the inquest, and he seems completely unruffled when he sees Norcross and his hired lackeys enter the courthouse. Rannah himself sometimes appears reluctant to be in harm's way. Instead of leaping upon the badmen at Mary's house and ripping them with his fangs the way Rin-Tin-Tin or Kazan would, the dog leaves to find his new friend Ted and get him to help.

Rin-Tin-Tin's son also starred in *Skull and Crown* in 1935. A Border Patrol officer in Arizona, Bob Franklin (Regis Toomey), anticipates the visit of his sister Babs (Lois January). She has just graduated from finishing school and they haven't seen one another in a year. Just before Babs' arrival at his cabin, he is called away to try to track down a vicious bandito, Zorro. He leaves his

roadster at the bus station with Rinty on guard so that Babs will have transportation. Arriving at the cabin, Babs is startled by the appearance of Zorro, who pretends to be a friend of Bob's. Rinty growls at him but the overly trusting girl tells him to be quiet, and the criminal kills her to get the keys to the vehicle for a fast getaway. Bob ejects Rinty from his cabin because he feels that the dog did not do his job protecting Babs. He resigns from the Border Patrol to go undercover and get revenge on Zorro. The owner of a lodge has his business commandeered by Zorro's mob and is forced to close it so they can use it as a hideout. The password is "skull and crown."

Franklin poses as a hoodlum named Rocky and introduces himself to King, a man who claims to work directly for the elusive Zorro. Rinty follows him silently and some of Zorro's men capture the dog and attempt to use him to pick out any undercover officers. Rinty wisely refuses to give Franklin away. "Well, if he's not your dog, you wouldn't care if we fill him full of lead, will you?" asks one thug. "Nahhh!" replies Franklin. However, when one criminal holds a gun to the animal's head, Franklin cannot bear it any longer, and confesses. The criminals now have what they want. No longer interested in Rinty, they put him in the kitchen, and Franklin is subdued with a rope.

Another undercover officer, this one a Customs agent, captures some of the men. Rinty breaks through a window where Franklin is tied to a chair. He chews the rope and Franklin has the satisfaction of beating Zorro just as the Border Patrol arrives, following the gang member used as a decoy. Zorro is really King in greasepaint and a Mexican bandito getup.

The character of Rinty, like Rannah in *Vengeance of Rannah*, fails to stop the villain when he arrives at the woman's door. This time, the girl dies. Rinty does not trust his own wonderful sixth sense; after all, he is supposed to be a dog

hero. He does perform heroic feats in the final 15 minutes, almost as an after-thought. The lynchpin of the story is Franklin, rather than Rinty. Rin-Tin-Tin serves in this film more as a disgraced former hero trying to regain his stature and win back his friends. Such scripts cast the dog as second banana and made it appear that the son of the great dog star was not much of a hero at all.

Rin-Tin-Tin, Jr., like Sr., had a secret cadre of stunt doubles known only to onlookers and persons "in the know."[8] Such a practice is standard now, and recommended by the humane organizations which oversee motion picture production. Lee Duncan was proud of the fact that his dog, and his stunt dogs, did all the stunts in their films and did not rely on special effects.

Rin-Tin-Tin III worked in WWII with his owner and trainer helping to train hundreds of dogs in the Army K-9 Corps.[9] After the war, he starred in one film, *The Return of Rin-Tin-Tin* (1947). His co-star was the very young Robert Blake, who played a Czech war orphan, Paul. Paul witnessed the death of his parents during a bombing raid on their town and goes to live with his rescuer, Mrs. Graham (Claudia Drake). She notices his unhappiness and wonders if Father Matthew (Donald Woods) might help. Paul befriends a dog that wanders

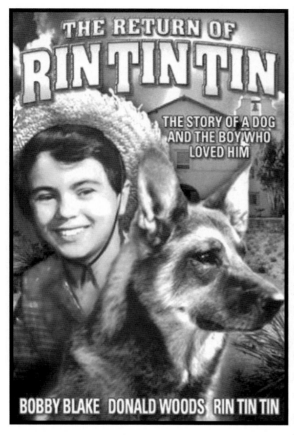

THE RETURN OF RIN TIN TIN

THE STORY OF A DOG AND THE BOY WHO LOVED HIM

BOBBY BLAKE   DONALD WOODS   RIN TIN TIN

into the mission barnyard. Rin-Tin-Tin, as it turns out, is a runaway, a champion German Shepherd sire worth over a thousand dollars. His owner, Melrose (Steve Pendleton), comes to the mission looking for him and Father Matthew reluctantly tells the boy to give him up. Losing another loved one crushes Paul. When the dog escapes the cruel kennel master and comes back to the mission, Paul conspires to hide him. The dog's presence is revealed during a small fire, which was accidentally started by the boy. The owner takes him back a second time, the dog attacks and escapes, and the owner hunts for his own dog now because it has seemingly become vicious. Rin-Tin-Tin saves the former owner from a mauling by another dog and Paul is allowed to keep Rin-Tin-Tin.

Rin-Tin-Tin serves to give the boy something to love after the loss of both of his parents, and helps Father Matthew in his quest to bring Paul out of his shell. There are really no surprises in the storyline. The film had a plot that would become very cliché in the decade ahead, and the picture failed to generate excitement for any merchandise featuring the grandson of Rin-Tin-Tin. The movie is readily available on DVD.

Rin-Tin-Tin IV, a great grandson of Duncan's original dog, was the star of the popular Screen Gems television series of the mid 1950s. *The Adventures of Rin-Tin-Tin* (1955-1959) was set in the Western frontier days and told the story of Rusty (Lee Aaker), a little boy whose parents had been killed. He went to live at Fort Apache, Arizona, and was adopted by the soldiers. Rin-Tin-Tin, the resident German Shepherd, becomes his loyal companion. The dog that played him was actually a son of Flame, and not trained extensively by Lee Duncan.

A typical episode of *The Adventures of Rin-Tin-Tin* was "O'Hara's Gold." The owner of the played-out Lost Frenchman Mine and his partner are looking for a rube to purchase the property. They plan to use a false fatal illness to win sympathy and a buyer. The Fort's comic relief, Sergeant Aloysius O'Hara (Joe Saw-

James Brown, Lee Aaker and Flame, Jr. starred in *The Adventures of Rin-Tin-Tin.*

yer) comes into possession of $25,000 that he inherited from a distant relative. Foolishly, he believes the men when they say there is more gold under the mining shack's foundations, and pays the entire fortune for the deed. The owner kills his accomplice because he hates to share and tosses the body into the mine. Rin-Tin-Tin smells trouble, and barks at Rusty and O'Hara to get them to enter the mine. The miner uses his horse to try to pull one of the supporting entrance timbers down. Rin-Tin-Tin leaps on him and stops him, and the others escape the mine just in time. O'Hara gets his money back and donates it to a charity. The dog is the only individual at Fort Apache who knows a villain when he sees one; fortunately, the troops are intelligent enough to listen to Rinty's warnings. Thank goodness for the dog!

The dog also acted alongside Esther Williams in MGM's biography of swimsuit pioneer Annette Kellerman, *Million Dollar Mermaid* (1952). As the film explains, Annette's great success in Broadway water ballets leads to a career in film during the very early years of motion pictures. An inexplicable bit of totally confusing fabrication takes place when Annette's former lover Sullivan (Victor Mature), accidentally meets her on a train going West to Los Angeles

The Dog Hero in Film

Won Ton Ton, with Art Carney (middle) and Bruce Dern (right) has a press conference in *Won Ton Ton, The Dog Who Saved Hollywood.*

with his new moneymaking scheme, a dog named Rin-Tin-Tin. Rin-Tin-Tin's owner and trainer, Lee Duncan, had no connection to Sullivan or to Annette Kellerman. Her motion picture career began before Rin-Tin-Tin was even born (and ended soon after).

The Rin-Tin-Tin line continues with new generations of purebred German Shepherd dogs. The Rin-Tin-Tin Fan Club in Crockett, Texas, is associated with ARF Foundation, which trains service dogs to help mentally handicapped children all over the United States. The Fan Club runs a Rin-Tin-Tin Museum in Latexo, Texas, boasting statuettes, books and other memorabilia. [10]

Rin-Tin-Tin's beneficial impact on the health of the motion picture industry was at once honored and satirized in the 1976 comedy *Won Ton Ton, the Dog Who Saved Hollywood.* Bruce Dern plays Grayson Potchuck and Madeline Kahn is Estie Del Ruth. The film has an all-star cast but is only available in Canada on videocassette or DVD. Estie Del Ruth, a lovely but broke young woman, wants a job in pictures, so she heads to Hollywood with a stray German Shepherd dog that has taken a liking to her. He is a one-person dog and Estie seems to have an amazing rapport with him. She becomes his trainer and promoter with the aid of a Hollywood tour guide and con artist Grayson Potchuck. [11]

Art Carney is producer J.J. Fromberg, who decides to take a chance on the girl and the dog. Hollywood is fascinated with both Estie and Won Ton Ton, and they become big stars at New Era Pictures. Potchuck is signed to direct their pictures, and he tries to use this opportunity to promote some concepts that have been popping into his mind. He pitches several film ideas to Fromberg. "There's this little girl in Kansas who is swept up into a cyclone. It takes

Won Ton Ton gives Estie (Madeline Kahn) a kiss in *Won Ton Ton.*

her to a magical land where she teams up with a scarecrow, a tin woodman and a lion to destroy a wicked witch." "Forget it!" the mogul replies. He is also not interested in Potchuck's pitch about a great white shark that eats tourists at a little New England oceanfront town. Won Ton Ton, meanwhile, becomes a huge star. He places his paw prints in cement in the famous forecourt of Grauman's Chinese Theater, an honor never bestowed on any real-life motion picture dog. In one scene spoofing the real Rin-Tin-Tin film *Tiger Rose*, Estie, portraying an Indian princess, noisily pulls an arrow out of the chest of her Cavalry lover. Estie and Won Ton Ton help Fromberg rake in the dough for a while, but their appeal is short lived. Estie tries to play her heroine roles straight, to no avail. Every character she portrays, from Indian princesses to farm girls, makes audiences laugh. Won Ton Ton's films are supposed to be serious.

Eventually, both of them are out of a job. Won Ton Ton is sold to a traveling show. Estie and Grayson rescue him from the road. Since her acting draws so many chortles and guffaws, Estie decides to return to Hollywood as a comedienne.

Said *New York Times* reviewer Richard Eder, "The gimmick is a trained German Shepherd named Won Ton Ton (Rin-Tin-Tin, believe it or not, is the reference) who makes a fortune and then fades from sight. The dog is all right. But Miss Kahn upstages him. It is because of her that Won Ton Ton is something more than a dog."[12]

CHAPTER FOUR
THE DOG HEROES
FIND THEIR VOICE

A very early sound serial with a dog hero was *The Sign of the Wolf* (Metropolitan Pictures, 1931).[1] Muro, a collie/German Shepherd mix, saved the day in this unintentionally comical serial starring one of Rin-Tin-Tin's costars from the silent days, Virginia Brown Faire. The story opens with Farnum, a businessman (Harry Todd) talking over some business with a fellow American in an India club. A man sells Farnum a puppy for 100 rupees, saying it is a sacred animal from the Temple of the Goddess of the Jewels, and that it will bring him luck.

At the same time, the swami of the temple demonstrates to the devotees the secret of some metal chains that, when added to ordinary sand, create rubies and emeralds. A stranger enters the temple and assassinates the swami. Prince Kuva (Edmund Cobb) must find Farnum, who has the sacred dog in his possession.

Years pass, and the sacred dog, named King, lives on a Southern California ranch with Farnum and his daughter Ruth (Virginia Brown Faire). Prince Kuva has followed the businessman to America. To communicate to Farnum the importance of giving up the secret of the chains and returning them to him, he uses blowpipes to send projectiles with messages attached crashing through the windows of the cabin. Farnum tries once to sell the chains to a wealthy businessman by the name of Winslow (Al Ferguson). Winslow has secretly hired henchmen to steal the chains from

Farnum's daughter. Throughout the remaining nine chapters, Farnum's chains are repeatedly stolen and King has to return them to him over and over. Farnum even buries the chains beneath a pile of small rocks in the forest to keep them from Wilcox's men, and this does seem to work, although a safety deposit box in a

bank would have worked marvels. The plot was typical lightheaded serial fare and the fight scenes are so badly choreographed that they induce belly laughs rather than excitement.

Here's a list of amusing things to look for:

1. Count how many times the bad guys visit the local dance hall in the course of two weeks and see the same dance hall patrons still seated at the same tables facing the same direction and wearing the same clothes.

2. Notice how many times Farnum looks dazed when yet another blow-pipe-propelled note crashes through a window.

3. Enjoy the most ridiculous scene in the serial in Episode 3, "The Wolf's Fangs." The crestfallen Ruth, having seen thieves steal the chains in the previous episode, prepares to leave the Winslow residence in her roadster. Friends Tom (Rex Lease) and Bud (Joe Bonomo) have arrived on horseback, albeit too late to prevent the robbery. Completely forgetting their horses, they ride off for home in the roadster! Later, we see the horses home safe and sound, a distance of 10 miles from the Wilcox mansion. Perhaps they caught the cross-town bus. King, meanwhile, leaps back into the mansion, grabs the chains from Winslow, and returns them to Ruth.

The crooks pursue the chains through six more episodes and imperil the stalwart King repeatedly until the final episode, "The Lost Secret." Farnum is captured by the bad guys and used as a lure to bring the dog and Ruth to a mountain cabin. The darkened cabin has a badger trap intended for Ruth hidden beneath some newspapers; she steps into the trap. A wire attached to the trap is set to knock over the lamp, setting the cabin ablaze. Fortunately, King is clever enough to chew through the rope tying Farnum's hands. He rescues his daughter and Tom arrives to be captured by the bad guys, now armed. Bud went to the sheriff some time ago (it's about time!) and the sheriff and his men arrive just as the villains get their hands on the hidden chains. Winslow arrives to try to pull a double cross on his compatriots, and is foiled by the sheriff. Prince Kuva at last explains that he is the guardian of the chains, and Farnum confesses his role in the theft of the marvelous chains. "But why didn't you force Farnum to give them up?" Tom wants to know. "My people do not believe in violence or death," he explains. "It is better to return them of his own accord." Farnum does so, and Kuva dissolves the chains in acid so that no one can covet them again. "The only things that are worth having are love and loyalty," says Kuva.

Lightning, grandson of Strongheart, had three starring vehicles in the mid-1930s. Lightning is not to be confused with Lightnin' the Police Dog, whose motion picture career ended just before the talkies began. Lightning starred in *A Dog of Flanders*, released by RKO in 1935. He also starred in *When Lightning*

Strikes (1934) and *Man's Best Friend* (1935). Strongheart's grandson meets the son of another 1920s film superstar in *When Lightning Strikes*. Francis X. Bushman, Jr., also known by his real name of Ralph Bushman, was the son of a silent era icon. Matt Caldwell (Francis X. Bushman, Jr.) and his father (Ralph Lewis) live in a cabin in a remote timbering area. The Broderick Lumber Company wants logging road access through the property whose lease is up for renewal. If the Caldwells do not renew, it reverts to the property owner, who can lease it to Broderick (J.P. McGowan), who would kill for that access. Mr. Caldwell gets a renewal and is on his way home when Broderick's ugly hired killers (Tom London and Blackie Whiteford) shoot him. He collapses while trying to escape but manages to give the lease to his dog Lightning to give to Matt. Lightning dashes off with the lease but is shot.

Lightning buries the lease and heads to the home of Matt's girlfriend Helen (Alice Dahl) for medical help. Matt comes home from a business trip only to have the marshal (Murdock McQuarrie) tell him that his father is missing and presumed dead. Helen, the marshal's daughter, found the injured Lightning in the woods and nursed him back to health. Unfortunately, Matt cannot find the lease. "It's all clear to me now," Matt thinks out loud. "Broderick's men shot

Lightning and took the lease from him." Lightning, now recovered, leads Matt to the lease. The hired killers set the cabin ablaze and the marshal arrests them and Broderick on the word of Matt and his dad.

Lightning, like Klondike in *The Law's Lash* (1925) and *The Sign of the Wolf* (1931) knows the identities of potential murderers and the location of a very valuable object that will resolve the problem faced by his human friends. If not for the canine detective, the Caldwells would have to abandon their home. This "hidden information known only to the dog" plot device was extremely common in the 1920s through the 1940s, but is seldom used today. J.P. McGowan, an actor in *When Lightning Strikes*, directed several Ranger films in the 1920s and was well acquainted with dog hero conventions.

Another feisty canine star was the light-tan coated German Shepherd named Flash, who continued his career into the late 1930s with Republic's lighthearted *Call the Mesquiteers* (1938). By now, he was at least 10 years old and a noticeably darker stunt dog doubled for him in running scenes.

Kazan starred in Principal Pictures Corporation's *Jaws of Justice* (1933) and *Ferocious Pal* (1934). Kazan had no tail, and is undoubtedly the only German Shepherd motion picture leading dog to be so un-endowed. He did start out with a tail when he began his career in films but unfortunately lost it in an accident. One of the promotional blurbs for *Jaws of Justice* read, "Kazan — the dog that out acts a man!" After viewing this film and evaluating the acting talents of Gene Toller as Kickabout Riley, Ruth Sullivan as Judy Dean, and his other human costars, one realizes that this statement is not just Hollywood hyperbole. Mounted Police Sergeant Kinkaid (Jack Perrin) leaves his dog with a young country girl named Judy Dean while he goes on a special assignment. A novelist named Boone Jackson (Robert Walker) offers to drive old Seeker Dean (Lafe McKee), Judy's father, from his mountain community

to a Canadian city. Dean is ready to stake a rich claim with the government. Jackson, intent on stealing directions to the gold, kills Dean by pushing him down a treacherous slope. Jackson returns to town with a story saying Dean had hitched a ride with some stranger into town. He then brazenly attempts to romance Dean's daughter Judy, who does not rebuff him but is more interested in finding out what happened to her father. The only individual who knows what has become of Seeker Dean is Kazan, who hates Boone Jackson, and the feeling is mutual. Mountie Kinkaid returns after a year to be reunited with his dog and to investigate Dean's disappearance. Deaf-mute Kickabout Riley is the only person Dean entrusted with a general location of the gold, and he presents Sergeant Kinkaid with a coded message written by Dean. Jackson finally decides to do something about Kazan's aggressive behavior toward him and shoots our stalwart champion. Fortunately, he is just grazed by the bullet and recovers quickly. Kazan brings Kinkaid one of Seeker Dean's shoes that he had been wearing the day he disappeared. Jackson, now a chief suspect, punches the Mountie when he confronts him. "You brute! Leave him alone!" Judy cries. With Kazan at her side, she breaks the code and learns that the motherlode is in a riverbed near a dam. Judy is overheard while thinking aloud— not the

The Dog Hero in Film

brightest thing to do with sneaky villains around, who are usually walking by an open window at the precise moment major discoveries are being made. Of course Hollywood conventions being what they are, that scoundrel Jackson hap-

pens by and hears Judy decipher the code. He assaults her, and Kazan leaps to her rescue. Jackson throws the dog against the cabin wall and flees to the dam with a box of dynamite. Judy faints and Kazan races after Jackson who has tied a rope to a tree and rappels down the steep slope to the riverbed. Kazan gnaws through the rope and then uses his paw to stamp out the lit dynamite fuse. Kinkaid arrives just in time to hug the heroine and find the villain's corpse. As in other films of the genre, Kazan finds the evidence that will convict the killer, continuing the tradition started by Wolfheart in *Wolfheart's Revenge* (1925) and *The Law's Lash* (1928). Kickabout Riley has a vague idea of the location of Seeker Dean's ore deposit, but lacks the confidence that the dog seems to have in ready supply.

Skippy, a wirehaired fox terrier, created a demand for the breed when he wowed audiences with his detective skill and general cuteness as Asta in *The Thin Man* (MGM, 1934). When we first meet urbane detective Nick Charles (William Powell) and his lovely and witty wife Nora (Myrna Loy), they are on vacation in New York City, having left San Francisco for a little time for themselves in their old hometown. Asta, their fox terrier, initially seems to be the most useless pet of the silver screen. "Sit down," Nick tells his furry companion—who immediately stands up. When commanded to stand—he sits.

In *The Thin Man* the now retired Nick is enjoying life with the effervescent Nora and her large inheritance. But when an old acquaintance goes missing, the man's daughter asks Nick for help. Inventor Clyde Wynant (Edward Ellis) is suspected of doing away with his mistress, who had stolen $50,000 from him. His pretty daughter Dorothy (Maureen O'Sullivan) fears the worst and appeals to Nick. Later, a minor hood breaks into Nick and Nora's hotel suite to also ask him for help but panics when the police show up on an unrelated matter. "You ratted on me!" he cries, and shoots Nick in the arm. Asta is no Rin-Tin-Tin as he sensibly cowers under the bed during the mayhem.

Skippy sometimes stole the show from Myrna Loy and William Powell in the *Thin Man* series.

Nick follows a hunch about going to Wynant's laboratory and he plans to take Asta with him. Nora tells Asta, "If you let anything happen to him, you'll never wag that tail again!" At the lab, the dog finds something under the floor. Nick uses a crowbar to reveal a hidden body covered over with concrete. The body has been there for months. Everyone thinks Wynant murdered the victim, because the skeleton is dressed in a suit with the initials "DWR," and Wynant is still nowhere in sight. Nick has his own suspicions about the real murderer. Nick and Nora give a dinner party and invite all the suspects — the police make sure the "guests" all attend. It turns out that Wynant is indeed dead and the killer is his mild-mannered assistant, who stole Wynant's invention and passed it off as his own.

Asta receives a hero's welcome from the press because, while Nick has a nose for crime, it was Asta who sniffed out the clues!

Although there were other canine hero films — *Inside Information* (1934) starring Tarzan the Police Dog, *Captured in Chinatown* and *Million Dollar Haul* (both 1935) and *The*

BERT STERNBACH
presents

A Police Melodrama

"MILLION DOLLAR HAUL"
with TARZAN THE POLICE DOG

and REED HOWES ~ JANET CHANDLER
WILLIAM FARNUM ~ ROBERT FRAZER
CREIGHTON HALE ~ JOHN INCE ~ VANCE CARROLL.
CHARLES KING ~ TOM LONDON
Distributed by STAGE *and* SCREEN PROD

Directed by AL HERMAN

Voice of Bugle Ann (1936), the dog hero cycle was winding down. However one more dog hero would emerge in that decade, and it occurred during the greatest year in movie history—1939. Many legendary films were produced in that one glorious year: *Gone With the Wind, Stagecoach, Gunga Din, Mr. Smith Goes to Washington, Dark Victory, Of Mice and Men, Son of Frankenstein, The Women, Goodbye Mr. Chips, Ninotchka, Wuthering Heights* and, of course, *The Wizard of Oz.*

Few moviegoers would recognize the name Terry, but everyone knows Toto, Dorothy's heroic pet in *The Wizard of Oz.* Dorothy Gale (Judy Garland) is a farm girl in Kansas in the 1930s living with her Aunt Em and Uncle Henry. Times are tough and the lonely Dorothy often feels in the way on the busy farm. And she is desperate when it looks like she may lose her only friend because the grumpy Elmira Gulch (Margaret Hamilton) is out for revenge when Dorothy's feisty Cairn terrier Toto (Terry) bites her on the leg. Miss Gulch confronts Dorothy's Auntie Em and Uncle Henry (Clara Blandick and Charlie Grapewin) to tell them she is going to take the dog to the sheriff to have him destroyed. Dorothy calls her a "wicked old witch" and watches, horrified, as her aunt and uncle allow Miss Gulch to ride off with Toto strapped in her bicycle basket.

The Dog Hero in Film

Judy Garland and Terry in *The Wizard of Oz*

Toto escapes and runs home to Dorothy, who quickly packs a small basket and runs away to protect her little dog. She meets Professor Marvel (Frank Morgan), a wise old charlatan who gazes into a crystal ball and advises her to return to Auntie Em. A big storm is brewing and the skies grow dark. Auntie Em calls for Dorothy but Henry pulls her into the storm shelter as a tornado rolls ever closer. They can't hear Dorothy pounding on the door. She returns to the house and is knocked unconscious by a flying window. The whole house is picked up by the whirling funnel cloud and dropped into the magical land of OZ. Unfortunately, or fortunately, depending on how you look at it, the house lands on the Wicked Witch of the East. Glinda, the Good Witch of the North (Billie Burke), and the Munchkins celebrate because the wicked witch is dead! But only the Wizard of OZ can help Dorothy get back home to Kansas.

As Dorothy follows the yellow brick road to OZ, she meets a Scarecrow (Ray Bolger), a Tin Man (Jack Haley), and the Cowardly Lion (Bert Lahr) who help her fend off attacks of the Wicked Witch of the West (Margaret Hamilton), who is the sister of the Wicked Witch of the East. She is determined to get the magical ruby slippers that Glinda has magically placed on Dorothy's feet. "I'll get you, my pretty—and your little dog, too!" The odd group of new friends

Jack Haley, Bert Lahr, Frank Morgan, Judy Garland, Ray Bolger and Terry, too!

nervously consults the imposing OZ, who appears to be a frightening green head. He tells them that he will help them if they secure the Witch of the West's broomstick. Her troop of flying monkeys captures Dorothy and Toto. The feisty pooch escapes the Witch's castle and finds Dorothy's friends and leads them to the Castle. Dorothy is rescued and the witch melted. The new heroes return to OZ and Toto reveals that the Great and Powerful OZ is just a harmless old charlatan. The Wizard, (Frank Morgan) Dorothy and Toto prepare to return home by balloon but Toto jumps out of Dorothy's arms to chase an OZ kitty, and Dorothy climbs out of the balloon basket to find him. The Wizard cannot stop the balloon and it leaves without Dorothy. Happily, Glinda tells Dorothy that she always had the power to go back to Kansas by clicking her heels together three times and saying "There's no place like home."

Dorothy wakes up to find herself in her own bed with her family and Toto, and learns there really is no place like home.

The Dog Hero in Film

The role Toto plays in The Wizard of OZ is critical to the entire storyline. Dorothy runs away to save him. Toto returns the favor when he escapes the witch and runs for help. It is Toto who exposes the false Wizard and, when he makes Dorothy miss her ride, he provides Dorothy with the opportunity to learn she always had the power to go home.

The Wizard of Oz was not considered a huge box office success, and might have faded into obscurity if not for its debut on television where, after repeated airings, it became a classic for children of all ages.

Belgian poster for *The Awful Truth*

Skippy, aka Asta, returned in *After the Thin Man* (MGM, 1936), *Another Thin Man* (MGM, 1939) and *Shadow of the Thin Man* (MGM, 1941). Skippy was much in demand and appeared in many popular comedies of the period: as Mr. Smith in Columbia's *The Awful Truth* (1937) and the mischievous bone-stealing George in RKO's *Bringing Up Baby* (1938). By the time *The Thin Man Goes Home* (MGM, 1944) went into production, Skippy was retired and another dog, this one actually named Asta, costarred with the principals.

When Nick wants to pay a visit to Sycamore Springs to see his folks, Mr. and Mrs. Charles park their boy in school and take the dog. But all is not entirely well in this idyllic suburban community. Nick's dad, Dr. Charles (Harry Davenport), seems to disapprove of his son's chosen profession, sneeringly calling him a policeman. He is also convinced that Nick is a lush. Nora has just the idea of how Nick can impress his father—by solving a local mystery. But are there any cases? Indeed, there are. It seems that Nick's arrival has galvanized several criminals into action.

Peter Berton (Ralph Brooks), hoping to speak with Nick, is shot dead just as he arrives at the Charles residence. Edgar Draque (Leon Ames) wants a certain painting Peter painted, one that depicts a local windmill and a collie. The gallery owner, Mr. Crump (Donald Meek), has promised it to Draques' wife, but Nora offered a better price, thinking it would please Nick, who had pointed out the windmill to her from their train. She does not know that the youth who was killed just outside her in-laws' home was the artist. Nick glances at it and says he always hated that windmill because it brings back bad memories of when his father whipped him there. Nora tells the housekeeper to burn it, but Nick's mother gives it to a charity bazaar to be held Saturday.

Nick questions the richest man in town, Sam Ronson (Minor Watson) who disliked Peter's attentions to his daughter. Dr. Charles objects to this questioning; he wants the man's money to finance his dream hospital. Asta knows there is something strange about that painting and helps Nick recover it from the shack of the town eccentric, Crazy Mary (Anne Revere). She had a connection to Peter Berton—he was her son by the tycoon. In one amusing scene, Nora trails her suspect, Nick's partner Brogan (Edward Brophy), to a pool hall.

William
POWELL
Myrna
LOY

TOGETHER AGAIN IN M·G·M's
RIOTOUS COMEDY

THE
THIN MAN
GOES
HOME

LUCILE WATSON   GLORIA DeHAVEN
ANNE REVERE
HELEN VINSON   HARRY DAVENPORT
LEON AMES   DONALD MEEK   EDWARD BROPHY

Metro Goldwyn-Mayer PICTURE

FOR
GENERAL
EXHIBITION

Draque approaches her and asks her if she still has that painting of the windmill. "My wife really wants it, and I'm willing to pay $500." "Fine," Nora replies. "I will call you and bring you the painting." She thinks fast to provide a diversion. Bellowing "You beast!" she pummels him with her purse. "That man insulted me!" she informs bar patrons, and hurries off to phone Nick to tell him of this new development. As it turns out, the painting is one of many that hide blueprints for a new propeller from the war plant where Peter had worked. Draque is an enemy agent who wants those plans. However, he is not the killer. The climax has Nick solving the case in his time tested way... bringing all the suspects together for dinner as in the original *The Thin Man* and then showing off his acumen, allowing his suspect to crack under the pressure and confess.

Asta helps Nick solve the case by scratching at that painting as though a dog biscuit is hidden inside. A.H. Weiler, film critic for *The New York Times*, raved over Asta: "If, at times, [the Charles'] erstwhile fast pace has been slowed to a walk, blame it on the script, which takes a long time introducing Nick to crime. But, with that cute canine, Asta, sniffing, barking and sitting up winningly in the proper places to assist in the proceedings, this newest of Metro's series spins a generally entertaining yarn fashioned along familiar plot lines."[2]

Song of the Thin Man (MGM, 1947) marked Asta's second appearance and the final film in the series.

Dog hero films experienced a resurgence in the mid 1940s, although they had never really disappeared from Westerns such as *Silver Stallion* (1941) with

Captain Boots. The most important canines of that time were Skippy, Asta, Pal (as Lassie), Ace, Flame and Friday. Friday was a distinctive-looking German Shepherd with a narrow, almost collie–like nose. He was the son of Flash, and was owned by William Frederick Steuer, who owned and trained both Flash and his sire. In MGM's *Eyes in the Night* (1942), Edward Arnold is legally blind detective Duncan Maclain, who has a seeing eye dog (Friday) and a valet Alistair (the irrepressible Mantan Moreland). He also has the benefit of a detective in training, Marty (Allen Jenkins), who drives him where he cannot readily walk. This tight and well acted drama about Nazi

spies posing as a drama troupe is unusual because it features a handicapped character and also showcases the athletic skills and intelligence of a Rin-Tin-Tin–like canine. Donna Reed shines in her first major role as Barbara Lawry, a conniving and controlling young woman who pits her stepmother Norma (Ann Harding) and her mother's former boyfriend against one another. Barbara is attracted to, but not in love with, an older man who had once had a fling with her mother.

Norma visits Maclain and wants him to kill her stepdaughter's new flame. He agrees to help her but with a more rea-

MGMs
The **HIDDEN EYE**

NEW ADVENTURES OF THE BLIND
DETECTIVE AND HIS SEEING EYE DOG

EDWARD ARNOLD
FRANCES RAFFERTY RAY COLLINS
PAUL LANGTON FRIDAY
Played by Himself
DIRECTED BY RICHARD WHORF PRODUCED BY ROBERT SISK A METRO-GOLDWYN-MAYER PICTURE

sonable request. She later calls him—it seems that the old flame was murdered moments before Norma visited his apartment. Barbara suspects her stepmother and gives her an ultimatum—leave the house or face murder charges.

That same night, Stephen Lawry (Reginald Denny) flies off to an official secret meeting concerning a chemical he has developed that will help the war effort. Meanwhile, all heck breaks loose at the Lawry household as the false drama troupe invades the house to try to force the Lawry to give them the formula, but he has already given it to the federal government.

Friday's best scene with Arnold occurs just after Maclain, posing as an obnoxiously drunk relative, enters the Lawry residence just as the Nazis are preparing to torture Lawry. Maclain punches out several Nazis, but is finally outnumbered. It's all up to the dog to run home and alert Marty and Alistair. Friday knocks over boxes so that he can climb them and escape through the window. Our devoted hero finds Alistair and Marty, the police rescue the Lawrys, and Barbara reconciles with her stepmother.

Friday proves to be an extension of Arnold's sensory ability as the dog really becomes his eyes. The quick thinking Friday and the intelligent Arnold together become one top-notch detective. The blind sleuth and his clever dog returned in the sequel, *The Hidden Eye* (1945).

A gigantic German Shepherd named Moose had a short but distinguished career in the early 1940s at Universal, making monster films. In *The Wolf Man* (1941), he portrayed the wolf that bit Larry Talbot (Lon Chaney, Jr.), young son

Lon Chaney, Jr. and Moose on the set of *Son of Dracula*

of the aristocrat Sir John Talbot (Claude Rains). The wolf is really a werewolf that returns to his human form with the waning phase of the moon to become the Gypsy Bela (Bela Lugosi). Larry kills the werewolf, but not before he is bitten and infected with dreaded lycanthropy. "Anyone who is bitten by a werewolf becomes a werewolf himself," Bela's mother Maleva (Maria Ouspenskaya) tells Talbot sorrowfully. She does not hate him for the deed, for she knows that there was no other help for her son. For a reason never explained, Larry takes the form of a wolf-like man instead of the fully realized wolf that Bela became. Moose is the only dog actor who has ever played a monster; in this case, a werewolf. His werewolf is the catalyst that ultimately destroys Larry.

The big Moose appeared one of the Universal Monster sequels—*Frankenstein Meets the Wolf Man* (1943). Here he portrays the sympathetic Bruno who belongs to Maleva. She is the only person who understands Larry's plight, and provides him with transportation and companionship as he seeks young Dr. Mannering (Patric Knowles), who has been studying Dr. Frankenstein's journal.

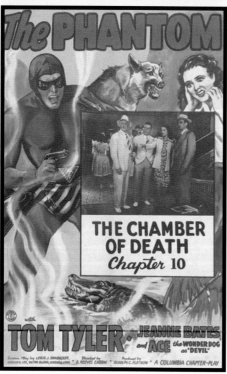

Larry believes that Dr. Frankenstein has a cure for lycanthropy and is the answer to Larry's misery. Bruno's role is minor in the best of Universal's WWII-era monster rallies.

Moose was a good friend to Lon Chaney, Jr., and accompanied him hunting and on the studio lot while he was filming *Son of Dracula* (1943). Moose's career ended when, on the studio lot, he was struck by a truck during the filming of *Cobra Woman* (1944).[3]

Ace was the biggest German Shepherd star of the 1940s. He was to be RKO's answer to Rin-Tin-Tin and was first introduced in *Blind Alibi* (1938). Working on Poverty Row, Ace made 16 films, including the 1943 serial *The Phantom,* as Devil, although he was uncredited. Ace also starred in *Almost a Gentleman* (1939), *The Rookie Cop* (1939), *War Dogs* (1942), *Silent Witness* (1943), *Adventures of Rusty* (1945) and *God's Country* (1946). His film career moved into fantasy films with Producers Releasing Corporation's peculiar horror effort *The Monster Maker* (1944).

Dr. Igor Markoff (J. Carrol Naish) and his laboratory assistant Maxine (Tala Birell) attend a recital given by famous pianist Anthony Lawrence (Ralph Morgan). In a box seat nearby are the daughter of the pianist, Pat Lawrence (Wanda McKay) and her fiancé Bob (Terry Frost). Pat is uncomfortably aware that Dr. Markoff is leering at her. Backstage, during her father's intermission Dr. Markoff enters. He apologizes to Pat and explains that his staring is due to her uncanny resemblance to his late

Ace and Tala Birell in *The Monster Maker*

wife. This is only the beginning of his obsession. Every day he sends the girl flowers and her father visits his office to tell him to stop. Unfortunately Dr. Markoff is not sane, nor is he Dr. Markoff. Several years earlier, he murdered the real Dr. Markoff, who was an eminent glandular specialist, stealing his formula and his name. The mad doctor then fled to America where he set up a well-staffed office including Maxine, his assistant, a big orderly named Steve (Glenn Strange), a German Shepherd (Ace), a laboratory pig and a gorilla (uncredited actor), which is kept in a cage. It is not clear how Markoff is using the gorilla in his plan to develop a cure for acromegaly. The unnamed German Shepherd is next in line to receive the injection and the experimental antidote.

Markoff wants to marry Pat, and her father's unexpected arrival plays right into his plans. He assaults Lawrence in feigned outrage when he threatens to call the police. When Lawrence comes to, Dr. Markoff asks him to forget this incident for the good of both of them. What Lawrence does not realize is that while unconscious he was injected with the compound that will give him acromegaly. Markoff plans to bargain with him—his daughter for the cure.

Markoff sends his gorilla goon to kidnap Pat. He watches gleefully as the gorilla ascends the outside stairway to her room. He does not see the German Shepherd quietly trot up the stairs behind the ape.

Markoff is shocked to find the gorilla sitting placidly in his cage and Maxine and the dog healthy and well. "Dr. Markoff," Maxine says casually, "Someone didn't lock the cage door last night and the gorilla escaped from his cage."

"No! Really? He could have killed someone."

"Yes, me! If the dog had not driven him back to his cage..."

"Steve has been negligent," declares the doctor. "I will discharge him immediately!" At that moment, Maxine sees that a pig that had been infected has returned to normal. The false physician has indeed developed a cure! Meanwhile, Anthony Lawrence reluctantly drives to the specialist's office. He has no other choice—Markoff is the only doctor who can give him any hope. Markoff's thug Steve straps him to a table. Markoff telephones Pat and asks her to come down to his office to authorize treatment. There is a catch—she must agree to marry him. Her father frees himself and struggles with the mad doctor. He shoots Markoff as Bob arrives to call the police. Maxine cures Lawrence, and the final shot shows the four of them enjoying another Lawrence piano recital.

The unnamed dog hero in *The Monster Maker* made the contrast between noble innocent animal and vile villain even more outstanding. Were it not for him, Maxine would likely be dead and unable to help the Lawrences; thus, the dog advanced the plot most ably.

Flame, often billed as Flame the Wonder Dog, starred in 16 pictures of the late 1940s including *My Dog Shep* and the Rusty series starring Ted Donaldson. Surviving films include *The Adventures of Rusty* (1945), *Rusty Saves*

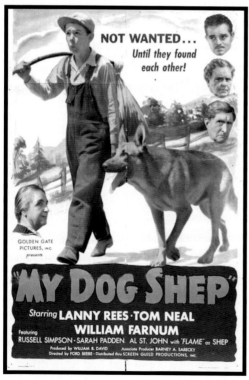

a Life (1949) and *Rusty's Birthday* (1949). Rusty gets into the sort of minor trouble that might be experienced by a pet dog in a middle class suburban environment, and Danny (Donaldson) always learns a lesson at the film's conclusion. In *Rusty's Birthday* (1949), one of the last of the series, Danny is a high schooler. His mother buys a new collar with identification for the family dog. "Put it on him, Danny, and see how it looks." Danny replies, "No, I will wait until his birthday. It's coming really soon." Of course something is going to happen to separate the dog from hearth and home. Rusty chases a would-be burglar out of the yard, leaps over the fence to get him, and follows him to a service station. A couple entices Rusty into their Airstream trailer after the burglar sells them Rusty. They carry him 100 miles before he runs away and heads home with the inadvertent help of an impoverished day laborer

and his children. Danny and his friends accuse the worker's boys of theft and, through numerous travails, Danny and the other youths learn a lesson about jumping to conclusions. Rusty is on hand to provide emotional support.

Old Yeller (1957) is possibly one of the most talked about American films, and much of its stature derives from the solid performances of the cast.

Jim Coates (Fess Parker) has to join a cattle drive, taking his steers to market for some needed cash. He leaves the homestead in the care of his wife Katie (Dorothy McGuire) and his oldest son Travis (Tommy Kirk). The youngest son, Arliss (Kevin Corcoran) is only six. A huge yellow stray happens on the scene, spooking the family mule and causing it to charge into a fence, making more work for Travis. He vows to shoot the dog if he sees it again. The dog shows up that evening, too full of food to care about Travis' opinion of him. His sated state is the natural result of having stolen some of the family's meat. Travis gets his rifle and Arliss screams at the top of his

WALT DISNEY presents OLD YELLER

lungs to their mother that Travis is trying to kill the dog. Mrs. Coates persuades Travis to calm down and let the dog have a chance at life.

Travis begins to warm to the idea of having the dog after Arliss taunts a bear cub a few days later and the big yellow mongrel drives off the angry mother. Old Yeller is quite adept at bringing in the family cow when she goes to the woods to have her calf. The dog's owner, Burn Sanderson (Chuck Connors), shows up for his cattle dog. Sanderson empathizes with the boys, and trades his dog to Arliss for a horned lizard and a home cooked meal from Mother. Before he leaves, Sanderson gives Travis a word of warning about the hydrophobia that has spread across the countryside and infected some of the local wildlife. "If you see a bobcat or other wild critter not running from you, or comin' at you, shoot it. If you wait until it bites you, you're too late."

A neighbor gives Travis bad advice about how to capture a live pig from a herd of feral hogs living in the forest by climbing a tree. The limb breaks and Travis falls into the herd. Old Yeller charges in and drives off the herd, only to be cut by their razor sharp tusks. The family nurses him back to health.

The neighbor's young daughter Lisbeth (Beverly Washburn) presents Travis with a pup from her dog's litter. Old Yeller is the pup's father, but she has

WALT DISNEY presents OLD YELLER TECHNICOLOR

kept this a secret because Old Yeller has a reputation in those parts as an egg thief and she likes Travis. Travis is not interested in the puppy. Sobbing at this rejection, Lisbeth gives the pup to Arliss. Just a month later, the family cow must be shot. Travis shoots a wolf about to attack Arliss as Old Yeller leaps upon it, and is relieved that his dog only received minor bites. Mrs. Coates was there and saw the wolf bite Old Yeller. "Travis, that wolf was mad. You know what we have to do now," his mother says gravely. Travis is horrified at what his mother suggests. "Ma, he saved Arliss' life! He saved all our lives! We cain't shoot him like he was nothing! Don't you understand?" His mother hasn't the heart to do it. They build a strong wooden stockade for Old Yeller. Two weeks go by and Travis is beginning to think that his dog has somehow managed to avoid the dreaded hydrophobia. Old Yeller snarls at Travis when he comes to feed him one night, and Travis' mother approaches the pen with a rifle to do the merciful thing. "You know we have to do it." She says to him compassionately.

"No, Ma. He was my dog. I'll do it."

WALT DISNEY presents OLD YELLER TECHNICOLOR

Re released by BUENA VISTA Distribution Co. Inc. © Walt Disney Productions

The next day Travis and Lisbeth bury Old Yeller in a field near the farm-house. His father comes home with a present for him; a horse he wanted. Katie tells her husband about the dog. He finds his oldest son placing rocks on the grave, and they sit on a log and he struggles to find the right words for Travis. "Now and then, for no good reason, life will haul off and knock a man flat. There's good and bad in life. We have to look for the good. If you look only for the bad and think about only that, then it's all bad. Do you understand what I'm trying to say, son?"

"Yes, sir," Travis says as he looks over at his father. They return to the house, where Arliss is playing with the pup Lisbeth had earlier given him. Travis picks up the puppy and manages a small smile when he licks his face.

The ending with the puppy, although helping to soften the traumatic blow, seems too pat. How many of us have lost a treasured pet, only to be told by well-meaning relatives or friends, "You can get another one." We surely can get another pet, but the loss is real, and so is the pain of watching a beloved friend become sicker despite our best efforts. Old Yeller makes the ultimate sacrifice protecting his pack, and no matter what Travis does, he knows it will haunt him. Many children lose animals over the course of their childhoods.

Most gravely ill or injured companion animals today visit a veterinarian and only in more rural areas does the retort of a rifle shot mean a death knell for the family pet.

Walt Disney was a leader in children's entertainment, but many of his most famous films contain dark elements a little frightening to younger viewers. Snow White eats a poisoned apple and falls to the floor of the Seven Dwarfs' cottage. A whale attacks Pinocchio. And hunters terrify animals in Bambi's beautiful forest.

Filmgoers have expressed concern over the years about the treatment of animals in *Old Yeller*, partly because it has received so much attention and because it involved much animal-on-animal violence. The American Humane Association monitored the film during all scenes with animals. A wolf prop and a cow prop were used for scenes involving contact between the dog and the other animals, and the wild pigs' tusks were rubber. Unfortunately, there was one casualty when Spike mauled the jackrabbit he was chasing in the scene introducing Old Yeller.

Spike played Old Yeller with much acting aplomb. Even though the Old Yeller character never again appeared in a motion picture, he became iconic.

Said *New York Times* film critic Howard Thompson wrote in his December 1957 review:

> Very happily, instead of isolating the little family on an island of sentimentality, in a nice, blunt, low-keyed manner the picture holds to reality, some of it quite strong for moppets. One scene of Master Kirk being attached by a pack of wild hogs is rough sledding. The climax, when his little brother attempts to free a snarling mad dog (yes, Old Yeller has to be shot) is plain frightening. However, it seems to us that most clear-eyed young-uns should be able to take these scenes unflinchingly. Especially with the straightforward honesty of Robert Stevenson's direction and the aura of family love that quietly caps the entire picture….As for Old Yeller himself, it's just too bad he couldn't fit into one Christmas stocking somewhere.

Vinyl records of the theme song were big sellers in the 1950s, and the dog's fame continues to market merchandise. In 2006 Inter-American Products of Cincinnati, Ohio, stocked stores with bags of "Disney's Old Yeller Chunky Dog Food."

Another popular dog hero of late 1950s theatrical films was named London. In the mid-1950s Chuck Eisenmann was a pitcher for the Chicago White Sox until a Korean War wound forced him to retired from major league baseball. For a while, he stayed at a rooming house in Los Angeles where he adopted a German Shepherd puppy, London, from a friend in town. Chuck had a dilemma. What was he going to do for a living? Eisenmann loved baseball too much to stop playing entirely. Both joined the Kearney, Nebraska, Irishmen minor league baseball team and Eisenmann and his dog entertained fellow players and the

audience when the dog would select the bat and the ball for his master. Eventually the dog's talents attracted the attention of *Life* magazine photographers who photographed one of the Irishmen arguing with the umpire during a contentious baseball game.[4] London then appeared on the popular *Art Linkletter's House Party* television series in 1957. He went to work shortly thereafter in the low-budget film *The Littlest Hobo* for Allied Artists in 1958, followed by *My Dog Buddy* (Columbia, 1960). The first film's popularity inspired a Canadian television series, which was broadcast from 1963 to 1965. It was one of the rare television series produced in color and aired in black and white.

Hobo feels the pull of the rail and he cannot stay in any one town long. The theme song, "Road Without End," was composed by Ronald Stein and sung by Randy Sparks. The show tended to romanticize the idea of a wandering dog. Anyone who works with dogs knows that homeless animals are never so sleek or well groomed. Hobo's character may have seemed familiar to 1960s audiences — he was the canine version of Buz and Tod, who cruised the countryside in their Corvette in *Route 66,* helping people along the way. To its credit, *The Littlest Hobo* was unafraid to show the seamy side of humanity. A particularly poignant episode, "The Silent Witness," has to do with the consequences of careless or cowardly actions. Handsome Sam Powers (Scott Peters) flirts with a young woman standing outside a hotel. When her boyfriend arrives he tells Sam to get lost. Sam's friend Bill (Larry Reynolds) intervenes, and counsels him on driving his car while he is still angry, reminding him that the next ticket he gets will mean that the police will suspend his license. Sam, still emotional over the encounter with the boyfriend, nods absently, tells his friend he will see him at work the next day, and roars off at a high speed in his convertible. The next scene shows the Littlest Hobo helping a nice elderly woman (Nan Stewart) by retrieving a purse she has dropped on the sidewalk. Sam's car tires screech as he speeds

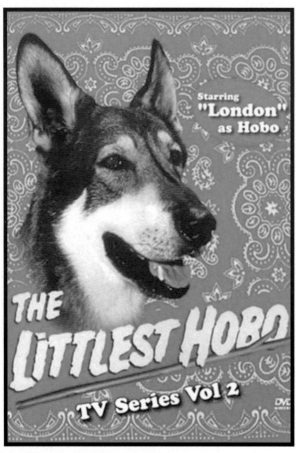

Starring
"London"
as Hobo

THE
LITTLEST HOBO

TV Series Vol 2

down the suburban street at twilight. His vehicle strikes her. The Littlest Hobo watches at a distance as the young man examines the woman's prone form, then gets into his car and flees the scene. The animal then runs to a house and barks to get the attention of the owners.

The next day the news of Mrs. Picketts' death appears in the newspaper. The Littlest Hobo drops a pale blue shawl that had belonged to the deceased on Sam's front porch. Sam decides to take drastic measures to rid himself of this silent witness. Hobo is too clever to eat the poisoned meat offered him and places it in a trash can. Hobo is a constant reminder of the terrible thing Sam has done, as the dog follows the young man to his job as a building construction superintendent. Sam becomes more and more irritable and paranoid. Bill stops him just as he is about to use a steel hammer to force the dog off scaffolding. Sam walks off the job and goes home to pack his suitcase. The Littlest Hobo heads back to Sam's house and raids the contents of his mailbox. Later, as Sam backs out of his driveway, he almost strikes a police patrol car. "Are you Samuel Powers?" one officer asks him.

"It-t-t was dark and I didn't see her until it was too late to stop. I wanted to help her…"

"So you're the one we've been looking for! Well, I'm glad to know that. We just came here to give you your mail that a dog brought to the police station."

"One Last Rose" is a far more lighthearted entry in the series. Harry Townes, a comedic character actor much in demand in the 1950s and early 1960s, plays Herman Eggles, a banker for the Hastings National Bank. Twenty-seven years of faithful service seem to have made no difference, as the manager keeps promoting younger employees to assistant manager positions. Recently, he has been telling his wife Beth (Carol Hill) that he is working at a florist delivery shop in the evenings so that they can afford a trip. He goes to the shop each evening for a single flower "for my girlfriends." Herman proceeds each night to a wooded lot and goes down on his hands and knees, entering a narrow sewer tunnel. Is this where Eggles meets the ladies? No, it's the bottom of the foundation for the bank. He plans to plant a stick of dynamite beneath the spot where the vault is located, get his reward and leave the country with his wife.

Hobo ingratiates himself with Beth and then follows Eggles to the sewer tunnel. "What are you doing here! Shooo!" Mr. Eggles says. Hobo snarls at him, and goes back and gets the wife, urging her to follow him. She discovers the tunnel and tells her husband she will refuse to go with him if he carries out this crime. Herman returns to the tunnel that night to collect his tools and seal off the entrance with mud. The dog follows. "Do you know how much money would fall on us if I blew one tiny hole up there?" Herman asks Hobo. He relents, and is about to leave when a monkey wrench is thrown into the works. Mr. Lilley (Tom Hill), the florist, enters the tunnel. "You're no ladies' man. I followed you because I knew you were up to something big and I want my cut!" he shouts.

Herman pretends to place the dynamite on the ceiling, and tells Lilley to back out. He obliges, and Herman outfoxes him by tossing the dynamite on the floor near the entrance. The next day, he returns to the florist shop and buys one more rose—for Beth. Herman's boss also promotes him. Hobo's work is done.

"Cry Wolf" is a tale of a nightclub singer, Marguerite Marlowe (Nita Talbot), who has not been drawing crowds to her latest gig. She cannot understand why, and tells the manager, "I packed them in in Redwood City!" He gives her a week notice. Marguerite meets Hobo and feeds him. He spends some time in her tiny first floor apartment behind a dance studio while she tries to figure out an answer to her unemployment woes. Calling her agent only gets some vague advice that she needs to get some publicity. Inspired by newspaper accounts of

The Littlest Hobo

a wave of stranglings, she tears her clothes and calls the police to give them a phony report of having driven off this strangler. The policemen and the newspaper reporter are highly skeptical of her report since she has a huge and fiercely barking dog, which she claims was asleep during the attack. They do not give her the kind of publicity she wants. An angry Marguerite yells at Hobo.

However, the real Strangler (Lloyd Berry) sees a tiny blurb in the paper about her attack and decides to make it real! While he breaks into her apartment, Marguerite calls the police, who take their time getting there. It's up to Hobo to save her and to hold her assailant in the alleyway until the police can arrive. A grateful and now successful Marguerite wants the big dog to be her permanent pet, but he will have none of the leash and collar she offers.

Eisenmann's biographer, David Malcolmson, quoted Eisenmann's philosophy of training London and his two sons: "Talk is better than commands.

Chuck directs them, not in obedience-school methods, but by speaking to them as people, and he gets a personal response from each."[5] He wrote several books on dog training techniques that were outside society's norms of the time. *Stop! Sit! and Think!* and *A Dog's Day in Court* emphasized careful observation of dog behavior and learning how to be positive toward the dog when training. Eisenmann lives today in Oregon.

Kelly, a large white German Shepherd owned and trained by Ernie Smith, played in tent shows and vaudeville houses before making it big in Hollywood. In *Kelly And Me* (1957) the talented pooch starred with Van Johnson who plays Len Carmody, a mediocre comedian working in vaudeville during the 1930s. Len is not very funny. He steals Kelly from his abusive owner Milo (Gregory Gay), and makes him part of his act. Now, he gets laughs.

Carmody decides to try Hollywood when he hears that many vaudevillians have made it big there. On the train trip, he and his dog encounter a beautiful stowaway named Mina (Piper Laurie). It happens that her father is Walter Van Runkel (Onslow Stevens), a Hollywood producer. Len and Kelly are cast in a film. The studio screens the film to a preview audience and finds that the audience likes Kelly best. Len is out and Kelly stays in. Angry at Kelly for what he sees as betrayal, Len shuns him and begins an affair

With AL RICKETTS

"KELLY AND ME" IS A CUTE FILM ABOUT A HAM (Van Johnson) and a hound (Kelly) who go from five-shows-a-day to five-grand-a-day on the dog's ability to make like Rin-Tin-Tin.

Johnson is a two-bit song-and-dance man lucky to get a phone booth booking until Kelly, abandoned by his owner, takes him in tow. As a team they skyrocket to fame, winding up in the Hollywood of the '30s when "talkies" were all the rage.

Almost overnight, Kelly becomes a star. They grind out picture after picture of Kelly saving a Mountie from a burning cabin, Kelly fighting Indians, Kelly in the frozen north—and the public clamors for more.

THROUGH IT ALL, Johnson gets shoved into the background. When—and if—he appears in one of Kelly's flicks the scriptwriter sees to it that he spends most of his time lying unconscious on the floor.

JOHNSON

Things are further complicated by the return of Kelly's owner, a swaggering Legree-type who desires to cash in on the dog's new career. With Johnson out of the picture, much heartstring-tugging must be done before man and dog can join in one of those "take it home" endings, while doing a Shuffle-off-to-Buffalo.

EX-CHORUS BOY JOHNSON DOES A nice job as the egotistical, razzmatazz grin-type that may not have killed vaude-ville but most certainly dealt it a crippling blow from which it never recovered.

As intended, however, he plays second-fido to Kelly, who remains top dog both in and out of the script. Kelly, a snow white german shepherd, manages to upstage the entire cast by being so doggonned natural.

In support: Martha Hyer as a no-talent movie queen and red-haired Piper Laurie, the gal who claimed to like flower petals for breakfast when she first came to Hollywood from Detroit.

KELLY

All told, "Kelly and Me" is strictly corn-off-the-cob, but it's digestible corn that the kiddies will enjoy and the adults can take with several grains of salt.

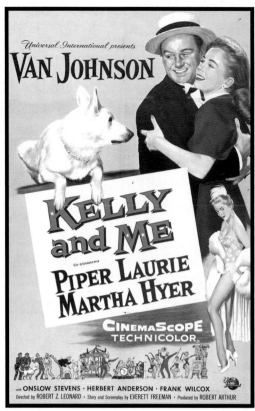

Universal International presents

VAN JOHNSON

KELLY and ME

Co-STARRING
PIPER LAURIE
MARTHA HYER

CINEMASCOPE
TECHNICOLOR.

with ONSLOW STEVENS · HERBERT ANDERSON · FRANK WILCOX
Directed by ROBERT Z. LEONARD · Story and Screenplay by EVERETT FREEMAN · Produced by ROBERT ARTHUR

with the producer's wife, Lucy (Martha Hyer). This results in his dismissal. Next, Kelly's original owner Milo comes back for him, claiming that Len never paid him for the dog and he still rightfully belongs to him. Milo then poses as his agent and trainer, but Kelly will not obey. Eventually the cruel owner reverts to his old ways and the dog runs away. Len comes to his senses when he finds out what has happened. He finds the dog at a San Francisco club. "Kelly, I'm so sorry, pal. Everything that happened was caused by my own stupidity."

Reviewer Al Ricketts in *Pacific Stars and Stripes* (June 6, 1957) remarked, "...he [Van Johnson] plays second-fido to Kelly, who remains top dog both in and out of the script. Kelly, a snow white german shepherd, manages to upstage the entire cast by being so doggonned natural."

In *Kelly and Me*, Kelly initially brings out the worst in Len when he eclipses the man in popularity in their first motion picture. Len's self-destructive tendencies come to the fore and he ruins any chances for a Hollywood career. Later, when he is a bottom feeder in the entertainment business once more, he realizes how much the dog loves him, and because of this, he becomes more mature in his approach to life. Here we see the dynamic of man who rescues dog who then rescues man, seen in several genre films such as *Clash of the Wolves* (1925).

Television and the intrepid dog hero were a match made in a Hollywood producer's dreams. *Sergeant Preston of the Yukon* aired from 1955 to 1958 and was one of the first television shows to be filmed in color—even though few homes of the time had color sets. It was shot mostly indoors on soundstages, but some Alaskan scenes were filmed at Big Bear Lake, California, a high country location just a few hours east of Los Angeles where a convincingly cold and snowy alpine environment was available during winter months.

Richard Simmons stars as Sgt. Preston. He, his horse and his Husky Yukon King, or "King" solve crimes and pursue fur smugglers, claim jumpers and murderers. Preston is an observant Mountie whose skills in deductive reasoning are in-

Richard Simmons and Yukon King

teresting for audiences of all ages. His loyal partner is the equally intelligent King, who never leaves his side. At the beginning of each episode the narrator reminds us that this series is about "Sergeant Preston of the Northwest Mounted Police with Yukon King, swiftest and strongest lead dog breaking the trail in the relentless pursuit of lawbreakers, in the wild days of the Yukon." Preston is kind but a little distant emotionally, and he needs King to help him express his warm side.

A typical episode was "Dog Race." Mayo Landing is a settlement known best for its annual 16-mile race. Preston wants to try out his sled team, since they have never raced before. A young man in the village, Dave (Wayne Mallory), wants to race, but his father (William Tannen) is against it, maintaining that he has seen men spend everything they had on teams, sleds, supplies and entry fees for racing: "It's a vice worse than gambling." Another sled driver, Adams (Edgar Dearing), brags that he will beat everyone. Adams has just acquired a husky

Elf Children's book featuring Yukon King.

The Dog Hero in Film

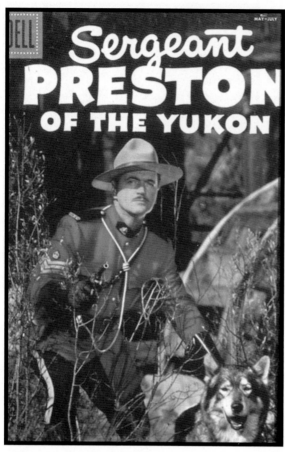

he names Savage, and both dog and man seem to live up to the name. Adams yells at the poor dog and treats him roughly. Old Hank Weber (Jason Johnson) is appalled. "No wonder he is savage, the way you treat him. I can tame him within two weeks," says Weber. "Care to put some money on that claim?" Adams taunts him. Weber goes so far as to bet $500. Young Dave succeeds in taming the dog in less than two days.

Meanwhile, Adams is experiencing tremendous pressure from the Dawson racing syndicate. The syndicate tells him to kill old Hank's lead dog. Adams really needs the dog race winnings and sends a man named Mantee to poison the dog. Weber surprises him in the act, and falls while trying to punch Mantee. The dog will recover, but both he and Weber are in no shape to race. Dave goes against his father's wishes and enters the race with the untried Savage in the lead. He wins the race, and Mantee is apprehended. Dave feels that Sgt. Preston would have won if not for the fact that one of his huskies injured a paw and had to be carried on the sled the rest of the race. He donates the winnings to Preston, who gives it to a local hospital.

Every episode ends successfully with Sgt. Preston hugging his canine friend and saying, "King, this case is closed!" Many episodes are available on DVD for animal lovers of every age.

In 1962, Warner Bros. returned to some of the seminal material of the original dog hero films and produced a lavish period drama based on the Albert

Payson Terhune book, *Lad, a Dog*. Peter Breck is Stephen Tremayne, a fictionalized version of author Terhune, and Peggy McCay is his wife Elizabeth in this film set in the early 1900s. The Tremaynes are plagued by a trespasser named Jackson White (Jack Daly), who insists that their farm Sunnybank, and the whole county, is his to hunt on because his family once owned the land. Elizabeth is afraid of him since Stephen once had Lad run him off.

A wealthy newcomer, Hamilcar Q. Glure (Carroll O'Connor) visits Sunnybank at the insistence of his handicapped young daughter Angela (Angela Cartwright). Angela has not walked since her mother was killed in a riding accident years ago. Angela is enraptured with Lad. Glure does not like dogs, he says, but he admires the many trophies the Tremaynes have on display, all won by the dog for sheep trials. "He's retired now," says Stephen. "Shows are a strain on a dog."

Stephen decides to breed Lad and brings home a female, Lady. Meanwhile, Glure donates the use of his estate for a Hampton show. Money will go to the Red Cross. Elizabeth is impressed by this gesture, and insists that Stephen take Lad out of retirement just this once for some conformation classes. She remains moved by what Glure did until the day of the actual show, when it is revealed that Glure paid $7,000 for a shepherding collie named Lochinvar II and has hired a trainer to coach him for the big show. In another display of unprofessional behavior, he has set the rules for all collie classes in such a restricted manner that the only dogs which are trained as working sheepdogs can enter. That leaves two dogs: Lochinvar II and Lad. Stephen is about to pick up Lad's leash and go home, but Elizabeth stops him. "Just because Mr. Glure is a poor sport, that does not mean that we must also be."

Lad is rusty, but he does a fair job in the trials. When it is Lochinvar II's turn, he does fine until the excited Glure, who insists on signaling the dog personally, puts the wrong end of his cigar in his mouth to free his hands for rapid hand signals. When he waves his hand to clear the smoke from his face,

HERE AT LAST FOR THE COUNTLESS MILLIONS WHO HAVE THRILLED TO IT-

Lad: A Dog

The wonderfully honest and honestly wonderful story of every child who ever wanted a dog. The most beloved of all Albert Payson Terhune's wonderful stories

PETER BRECK | PEGGY McCAY | CARROLL O'CONNOR ANGELA CARTWRIGHT | LAD

Screenplay by LILLIE HAYWARD and ROBERTA O. HODES · Produced by MAX J. ROSENBERG · Directed by ARAM AVAKIAN and LESLIE H. MARTINSON

TECHNICOLOR® From WARNER BROS.

it confuses Lochinvar II. He sits down, and Glure goes into the ring, trying to get him to continue. Being too close disqualifies him.

Angela is secretly glad Lad won and insists on another visit to Sunnybank. Lady is going to have Lad's puppies and Elizabeth promises her one. Angela's nurse Hilda (Alice Pearce) wheels her wheelchair down to the lake's edge. A rattlesnake hidden in the sedges is startled by the child and strikes at her. Lad grabs the snake and keeps it away; in the fracas he is bitten. Hilda beats the dog with her umbrella, convinced that he is biting at Angela. She screams at Hilda to stop, and stands up and walks over to her to try to grab the umbrella. Lad flees into the woods.

Mr. Glure happens upon the scene and sees his daughter walking once more. The Tremaynes search the woods for Lad. He has gone to the swamp to lie quietly in mud in an instinctive move to draw the poison from his wound. He returns a few days later to find that Lady has had her litter. There are only two pups. One has already been named Wolf. Angela picks out one and names it Little Lad.

But the final credits are not ready to roll just yet. Jackson White has not finished making life miserable for the Tremaynes, whom he now hates with a passion for driving him off what he considers his land. He enters the barn where Lady and her pups stay. Stephen and Lad, out with Stephen's horse, do not see

Carroll O'Connor, Maurice Dallimore, Angela Cartwright and Lad

what has happened until the barn is very nearly engulfed in flames. Elizabeth runs out to try to save the dogs and is successful in saving only Wolf. She is knocked unconscious by a falling pole and Lad and Stephen keep constant vigil at her bedside until she wakes.

Hamilcar Glure must break the news to his young daughter that Little Lad has died, and she takes it very hard. Meanwhile, White attempts to set the Tremayne home on fire and finish them off once and for all. Stephen and Lad overcome him and hold him for the police.

Angela comes to Sunnybank to visit Elizabeth after she has recovered. Elizabeth offers her Wolf, but she refuses to have anything to do with him. Lad tries to interest her in playing a game with a stuffed toy fox. The older collie leads her to a spot on the lawn where Wolf is waiting for her, having been placed there by her father and the Tremaynes. Angela becomes angry at the deception, screeches, and throws the toy at Wolf. Wolf is startled and runs off toward the long estate driveway. The family chauffeur, alarmed, drives over to see what is the matter with Angela, and in doing so almost hits the puppy. Angela sees the toy fox between the wheels of the car and thinks she has sent the pup to its death.

Tearfully, she cries out, "I'm sorry, Wolf! I'm sorry!" She finds to her great relief that he is safe. She then promises that she will train him and he will be her own special dog. "Please stay." The Tremaynes and Mr. Glure's plan worked.

Albert Payson Terhune is commonly and erroneously credited with having written the novel *Lassie Come Home*, which inspired the films and television series about the beloved fictional dog. (The next chapter will examine this dog's impact on film and television.)

Several other acting pooches appeared onscreen in the late 1940s and 1950s: a screwball comedy with Carole Landis as the owner of a Doberman called *It Shouldn't Happen to a Dog* (1946); a rare serious film from comic Joe E. Brown, *The Tender Years* (1948), that tackled the subject of cruel dog fighting and was supported by local chapters of the Humane Society and SPCAs; and finally the odd Universal film *Edge of Hell* (1956) about a man who must sell his beloved dog, but they meet again in heaven.

LASSIE COMES ALONG

Lassie, a member of the breed known as the rough collie, was originally the subject of *Lassie Come Home*, a novel written by Scottish author Eric Knight. Lassie's major attributes as a character are her steadfastness and intelligence. Unlike Strongheart, Benji and Rin-Tin-Tin, whose real names appeared in the marquee lights, there was no real dog in any Lassie films named Lassie until 1994. The first film Lassie was a male named Pal. Rudd Weatherwax came into possession of the animal in the 1940s when he owned a dog kennel and training facility in the Los Angeles area. Pal was a drop-off that the owner decided he did not want to claim. Instead of paying his kennel bill, Pal's owner gave him to Weatherwax. Pal had some behavior problems, but Weatherwax was able to retrain him for pictures. One trait he never lost was his fondness for chasing motorcycles, a behavior that got him on his former owner's bad side in the first place. Weatherwax turned his quirk into an asset by making recommendations to several directors to incorporate these kinds of scenes into the dog's films.[1]

"You'll have to take her back! She's not ours any more!"

A Metro-Goldwyn-Mayer picture

The Dog Hero in Film

"We must save her. She's come a long way and she's been through almost more than she can bear."

a Metro Goldwyn-Mayer picture

His first film was MGM's *Lassie Come Home* (1943) starring Roddy Mc-Dowall as Joe Carraclough and Elsa Lanchester as Mrs. Carraclough. The novel was more or less faithfully adapted for the screen. Every day, Lassie, a dog of Yorkshire, leaves the house at 3:48 to head over to school. There, she waits for school to let out at 4 o'clock so that she can accompany her young master Joe home. The family falls on hard times during the Depression and their expensive purebred collie, Lassie, is sold to a wealthy neighbor to pay bills.

Mr. Carraclough (Donald Crisp) is out of work for many long weeks after the dog has been sold to the Duke of Rudling (Nigel Bruce), and they are running out of money even to buy decent food. "Joe told me that he thinks Lassie brought luck to us," Carraclough's wife mentions to him. "He is a good lad, you know."

Lassie is not doing well at the big kennel where many other purebred collies live. This fact is not lost on the Duke's 9-year-old granddaughter, Priscilla (Elizabeth Taylor). Lassie digs out and returns home, only to be hauled back by the kennel master, Hynes (J. Pat O'Malley). She is taken to the Duke's Scottish estate, hundreds of miles away. The second time she escapes it is with the help of Priscilla, who conveniently leaves the gate to the estate open as she and her

grandfather prepare to take a leisurely canter on their horses. Lassie travels across the breadth of Scotland, using her homing ability. Shepherds almost kill her when they mistake her for a marauding sheep predator. She gets away after driving off their large dog. Her swim across the Tweed River that separates Scotland from Yorkshire is a dramatic highlight of the film. Exhausted, Lassie collapses in front of a Yorkshire cottage owned by an elderly couple. Soaked by a thunderstorm, she is very ill from exposure. The couple (Ben Webster and Dame May Whitty) nurse her back to health.

Each afternoon, at 3:48, Lassie becomes agitated. She paws at the door, and the wise old lady realizes that she did not come to them to stay—there is somewhere else she needs to be. "She is just too polite to run out the minute we open the door. We have to give her permission." Mrs. Fadden explains to her husband. They grant her permission to leave and she does so. Lassie gets a ride part way in a caravan belonging to a tinker by the name of Rowlie (Edmund Gwenn). She drives off two robbers that intend to bludgeon him and take his earnings. Lassie saves him and his money, but his own little terrier is killed helping Lassie fight off the criminals.

Rowlie is especially sad to have to say goodbye to "Your Majesty," as he calls her, now that his own dog has died. After being injured once more, this time when escaping dogcatchers in a nearby town, Lassie arrives at the Carraclough home. Her feet are torn and bleeding. The Duke of Rudling arrives almost within minutes to inquire whether they have seen his dog Lassie. Seeing the bedraggled, underweight dog that lies on the floor, he tells the family that this is not his dog. The gruff but kind Duke is no fool. He realizes that there is a better way to handle the situation than to simply take the dog back with him. He offers Mr. Carraclough a job working as kennel manager since he let the incompetent Hynes go. That way, he gets to enter Lassie in dog shows and even breed her.

Bosley Crowther of *The New York Times* was enthusiastic about the film.

> Oftentimes, animal pictures make the unhappy mistake of attributing almost human rationalization to simple four-footed beasts. An outstanding virtue of this picture is that it does nothing of the sort. It treats the dog as an animal whose loyalty is all the more wondrous and appealing because it is simple and free of human wile. The homing instinct of Lassie, her perseverance to get back to the boy she loves, is beautiful because it is indicative of emotion that is primary and pure. The human actors in this picture are excellent in their simple roles....But it is really the collie, Lassie, which is the most remarkable performer in the film. The beauty of this dog and her responsiveness go far to make the picture a thorough delight.

Son of Lassie (1945) was the sequel to *Lassie Come Home*. It fast forwards the story to WWII and the now grown-up Joe Carraclough (Peter Lawford).

Laddie, Lassie's son, serves with his master in wartime, but not by the young man's choice. In fact, Laddie's presence causes difficulties for his master, a pilot for the Royal Air Force. He breaks loose from his far off home in the Scottish countryside and seeks out Joe. Here we find that June Lockhart was involved with Lassie more than 10 years before her famous role in the television series. She portrayed the grown-up version of the character Elizabeth Taylor played in the first film. The dogs in the MGM series were owned and trained by the Weatherwax family which had been involved with the motion picture industry since 1913.[2]

The New York Times did not heap praises on this film:

> Comparisons are odious but sometimes inevitable, and since Metro's *Son of Lassie* officially is proclaimed a sequel to *Lassie Come Home*, it is only fair to point out that the newcomer falls short of being a worthy heir to a champion. For the dog adventure which arrived at Loew's Criterion on Saturday subordinates the warm and tender sentiment which characterized its predecessor to a topical and highly improbable plot....once

The Dog Hero in Film

Slowly recognition came to him... the girl he had bitten... was the same girl who had befriended him as a puppy.

LASSIE
COURAGE
of LASSIE
in Technicolor
ELIZABETH TAYLOR
FRANK MORGAN · TOM DRAKE

again, the story is concerned basically with a beautiful collie's devotion to his master. Gorgeous but apparently not blessed with too much sagacity, Laddie trots some 40 miles from home to be with Joe Carraclough, RAF flyer. A great canine for traveling great distances, Laddie braves snipers, bombings, hand grenades, a ferocious police dog, glaciers and raging rapids to seek out his adoring owner. It is this blind, indomitable love which nearly traps his master when the undiscerning Laddie leads the enemy soldier-searchers to his hideout. And it is as much the self-sacrificing underground and stamina which serve finally to bring the two together for their ultimate escape to England. [3]

Son of Lassie was followed by *Courage of Lassie*, released in 1946. The film starred Elizabeth Taylor as Kathie Merrick, Frank Morgan as Harry MacBain and Tom Drake as Sergeant Smitty. Lassie plays Bill, a dog that lives in the wild after becoming separated from his family. He is eventually adopted by Kathie

"This dog isn't vicious... He's been changed by the war, just as many men have been changed. All he needs is a chance!"

LASSIE in COURAGE of LASSIE in Technicolor ELIZABETH TAYLOR FRANK MORGAN · TOM DRAK A METRO-GOLDWYN-MAYER PICTURE

and is then drafted into the K-9 Corps. The poor battle fatigued Bill returns home where his is considered vicious and put on trail for his life.

In *Hills of Home* (1948), the fourth Lassie feature, Edmund Gwenn is reunited with Lassie, this time playing Dr. William MacLure. The previous year Gwenn had earned high praise, not to mention an Academy Award and Golden Globe, for his performance as Santa Claus in 1947's *Miracle on 34th Street*. Tom Drake also returned to make another appearance with the famous collie, and up and coming young actress Janet Leigh portrayed Margit Mitchell. The cast also includes several famous British actors, including Reginald Owen and Alan Napier. The story focuses on the trials and tribulations

HILLS OF HOME EDMUND GWENN · DONALD CRISP TOM DRAKE · JANET LEIGH AND LASSIE A METRO-GOLDWYN-MAYER PICTURE

5—An emergency call—and the doctor, his faithful collie and his horse brave the winter storm to answer it!

FOR GENERAL EXHIBITION

HILLS OF HOME

EDMUND GWENN · DONALD CRISP
TOM DRAKE · JANET LEIGH
AND LASSIE
A METRO-GOLDWYN-MAYER PICTURE

4—Through raging blizzards, Lass brings help to her stricken master!

FOR GENERAL EXHIBITIO

LASSIE
THE PAINTED HILLS
IN TECHNICOLOR
PAUL KELLY
BRUCE COWLING
GARY GRAY

of a Scottish doctor and his dog Pal. Although Pal is afraid of water, the brave collie swims across a river to save MacLure.

Challenge to Lassie (1949) finds the dog reunited with Gwenn, Owen and Napier. The film was based on the true story of Greyfriars Bobby, a dog that remained by his master's grave in Edinburgh for 14 years until the dog also passed away. When his beloved owner dies, Pal (Lassie) must be saved from a judge who thinks he should be put down.

The final entry in this Lassie series is 1951's *Adventures in the Goldrush* starring Paul Kelly. The film is also known as *The Painted Hills*.

"Who among us really knows what is in the heart of a dog?" muses the narrator as the camera pans across mountain scene at the beginning of *The Painted Hills* (1951). The title for *The Painted Hills* should have been *The Painted Hills: Now It's Personal!* Pal, as a female collie named Shep, goes on a mission of vengeance against a man who murdered her master Jonathan Harvey (Paul Kelly) to steal his gold. Then the killer, Lin Taylor (Bruce Cowling), attempts to poison Shep so she will cause him no further trouble. Native Americans find her and treat the suffering pup with herbs. When recovered, Shep finds young Tommy (Gary Gray), who had cared for the dog.

Tommy knows from the dog's sudden aggressive behavior toward Taylor that the man is lying about the whereabouts of the old prospector. He also suspects that Taylor tried to poison Shep, and tries to tell the local minister and others. The Reverend is not interested and does not take the word of children seriously. Taylor decides it is time to get rid of Tommy, just as he tried to get rid of the collie. However, Shep, the angel of protection, attacks Taylor with enthusiasm. The salivating animal drives him to the edge of a cliff where he falls to his death. Viewers who grew up watching reruns of Lassie on television might have a hard time seeing a collie as an attacker, even with just motivation.

The Painted Hills is advertised as starring Lassie, when it really stars the animal that played her. Chester M. Franklin, director of many a Rin-Tin-Tin and Peter the Great drama, produced *The Painted Hills*. It was to be his last dog hero film and MGM's last Lassie feature. Lassie's next appearance would be on television.

Pal starred in the premiere episode of *Lassie* in 1954, but his son took over afterward. The series won an Emmy for best children's program in 1956. Lassie episodes promoted the values of bravery, honor, environmental conservation and humane treatment of animals. In the early years,

Lassie and Tommy Rettig

Lassie is a companion to Jeff Miller (Tommy Rettig), a boy living on a farm somewhere in the United States, and his adventures with his friends Harry and Porky.

Jeff is a flawed, yet likeable child who tends to be petulant and stubborn toward his mother Ellen (Jan Clayton) and his Gramps (George Cleveland), especially when he feels that adults do not grant him credibility. The premiere episode "Inheritance" demonstrates the struggles of a child to be listened to and believed. An elderly neighbor dies suddenly, and Jeff and his mother are asked to come to the reading of the will. Jeff inherits the old man's dog Lassie,

Original 1954 cast: Gramps (George Cleveland), Doc (Arthur Space), Ellen Miller (Jan Clayton), Jeff (Tommy Rettig) and Lassie and Pokey

relatives inherit the house, and there is some discussion about missing money. The old man's former handyman asks the relatives if he can stay at the place for a few more days while he looks for a new place to live. They consent to his remaining for a week. Lassie keeps returning to his old home and Jeff is heartbroken. Nevertheless, he enters the house illegally to try to convince Lassie to come back with him. He finds her sitting on the corner of the fireplace bricks as though waiting for the old man. The handyman threatens them. During the fracas, Jeff accidentally dislodges a brick and finds the stash of bills that the handyman has been seeking. The man flees to a boat. Jeff must convince the sheriff to follow. Lassie stops the criminal but almost drowns in the process. In the final scene, Lassie leaps out of the Miller car as they arrive home, and seems determined to head back to the empty house of her former master. "Jeff, sweetie, we cannot force Lassie to stay here if she doesn't want to," Mrs. Miller tells a tearful Jeff. Lassie then pauses in the middle of the road, seemingly making up her mind. Finally, she comes to Jeff's side.

In "Lassie's Pups," Jeff gets to demonstrate his better qualities. During a bad thunderstorm, Lassie is struggling with the process of giving birth. There is a fire in the community, and Gramps, a volunteer firefighter, needs to use the family car. Things worsen when the storm knocks out the telephone service. By one o'clock in the morning the storm has finally abated, but Lassie is having real trouble. Jeff pleads with his mother to allow him to ride his bike five miles on dark country roads to get the veterinary. Although Jeff's bike is wrecked when making a wrong turn in the dark and he has to walk quite a distance,

"Lassie's Pups"

he finally makes it. Jeff's courage and determination saves his pal Lassie.

As Jeff ages, he matures and learns. In "The Tree House," Jeff and Porky (Joey D. Viera) make a blood brother pact ("just like the Indians"). Their latest project is a tree house, and they talk Gramps into helping them build it. They and their dogs decide to spend the night in the tree house. They use a clever dog elevator operated by a pulley system to bring up their pets. The first night in the tree house is a disaster, because Porky's hound Pokey starts to howl. Jeff demands that Porky take Pokey down and tie him up at the base of the tree, and he refuses. He then tells Porky and Pokey to get out of his tree house. "I'll get even with you!" Porky shouts as he leaves, and Jeff and Lassie come down from the tree house—it's no fun anymore. They find the tree house interior a shambles the next day. Porky says he had slept in his parents' barn, too ashamed to tell them that he had had a fight with Jeff. He insists that he didn't do it. Jeff remembers Porky's parting words the night before. The mystery is solved when Gramps and Jeff find the real culprit—a bear attracted by food left by the boys in the tree house.

In 1959 Pal Junior contracted cancer and was replaced. He did recover but never worked on a set again. Spook, another son of Pal, was rushed into train-

Jon Provost, Hugh Reilly, June Lockhart, George Chandler (1955-1959) and Lassie took over from 1958-1964.

ing. Spook became averse to working in television after he witnessed an accident on the set. Spook, despite his lack of enthusiasm for television production, sometimes showed up as Lassie in season eight, and viewers were beginning to notice that two different dogs were playing Lassie. Several letters from fans complained that "the real Lassie" was being short-changed. Baby, Spook's brother, filled in for him and eventually replaced Spook toward the end of the seventh season. Baby played Lassie for the longest period of any of the Lassies, from 1960 to 1968. Jon Provost, as orphaned Timmy Martin, joined the cast in 1957. The unexpected passing in 1957 of George Cleveland, who had played Gramps, caused the scriptwriters to re-think the entire series. They solved the problem by working his death into the storyline.

The death of Gramps forces Jeff's mother, a widow, to sell the farm and move to the city. Because they have to move to a small apartment, Jeff gives Lassie to the adopted parents of Timmy, the Martins.[4] New owners Ruth Martin (Cloris Leachman) and her husband Paul (Hugh Reilly) adopt the dog. The next season June Lockhart replaced Leachman.

Timmy was younger that Jeff, so only occasionally did the script give him something heroic to do, as in the 1960 season episode "The Grasshopper and the Ant." Timmy tells his father about a huge nest of locusts, so Martin informs the farmers at the local Grange meeting and they destroy the nest. Another such episode is one from 1962, "Home Within a Home," when he tries to save some wildlife living in his friend Cully's (Andy Clyde's) barn. A new gas line

is coming through the farm and the structure is to be torn down. His teacher tells him, "Take pictures and write to the local newspaper to get the law to make an exception this one time." The county does.

In 1963 the Martin family and Lassie moved to the big screen for *Lassie's Great Adventure.*

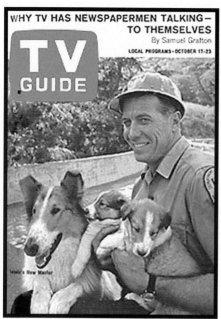

Lassie **with Robert Bray**

Lassie storylines unfortunately moved into melodrama and cliché as the years passed. Lassie's companion Timmy began getting much too careless. Timmy's blunders include hunting an escaped tiger with cap gun and butterfly net, releasing a dog diagnosed with rabies, and becoming trapped on a ledge. Lassie's purpose in the program is to protect Timmy from his own incompetence—to be a guardian angel. Eventually *Lassie* became a target for satire. *Mad Magazine* lampooned the series. Even *The Flintstones* (1965) satirized *Lassie* with "Sassie," an overly melodramatic show aired on Bedrock television. In "Sassie," the noble dog saves her rag-clothed family from starvation and finds money for them.

To revamp the series, in 1964, the Martins moved to Australia and gave Lassie to a ranger with the United States Forest Service, Corey Stuart (Robert Bray), a middle-aged bachelor. Lassie accompanies Stuart on his fire patrols in California.

An accident suffered by actor Robert Bray forced him to quit the series and the storyline changed to accommodate his departure. The 1968 episode "Holocaust" explains Bray's departure from the series. Corey and a fellow ranger are seriously burned in a firestorm they are fighting in the California mountains near Santa Clarita. Despite their fire protection gear, they are near death. Lassie and two other rangers come to see them in the hospital. One of the men takes her with him to Alaska while Corey is recuperating from his injuries.

Lassie now lives with two young rangers, Scott Turner (Jed Allan) and Bob Erickson (Jack DeMave). For a season, she helps them deal with the kind of situations real rangers encounter: dune and beach erosion, campground delinquents, and the like. Lassie's travels take her back to California. Along the way, Lassie manages (at the presumed age of 16 years!) to give birth to a fine litter of purebred collie puppies. The father, Duke, is nowhere in evidence, making Lassie one of TV's first single mothers, and a further indication of the erosion of the stable family theme that was the hallmark of the earlier years of the television series. For a while, she lives with a deaf girl named Lucy Baker (Pamelyn Ferdin). During the 1973 season, the dog has no permanent owner. She roams the countryside, helping people solve their problems — never staying with anyone for more than a week or two. Audiences must have found this to be a tired reworking of *The Littlest Hobo*, since ratings were down and cancellation

POST

In 1963 *The Saturday Evening Post* did a cover story on Lassie.

dogged the series. Rudd Weatherwax was involved with the training and supervision of all dogs used in the 20 years that the series was on the air. William Beaudine, whose career in motion pictures went back to the 1910s, directed the series. He directed greats like W.C. Fields and Mary Pickford, and was known as the guy who would always bring in a picture on budget. Classic Media offers 18 episodes from the television series, six from each decade, in a three-DVD set entitled *Lassie—Celebrating 50 Years of Love*.

Lassie returned in 1994 as a contemporary drama. Thomas Guiry starred as Matt Turner, the unhappy young son of Steve Turner (Jon Tenney). Brittany Boyd was his younger sister Jennifer. This Lassie is a dog totally unrelated to the original Lassie of the old MGM films or TV series.

However, this series does acknowledge the original Lassie series. Jennifer loves the *Lassie* reruns, but her brother changes the channel to superhero cartoons whenever he sees the familiar black and white images of the television dog. Their widower father has just remarried and they are packing to move

from their home in Baltimore to his late wife's family farm in the mountains of Virginia. On the trip they are delayed by a terrible automobile accident. During a storm a truck carrying sheep collides with a small car. The sheep are scattered and a bewildered looking collie watches as paramedics take the driver of the truck to the hospital. The dog fascinates eight-year-old Jennifer, who insists that this is the famed collie of the television series. "That's not Lassie! Lassie doesn't exist!" Matt insists. The collie wants to come with them, so the Turners reluctantly let her accompany them to the farm. Matt sulks so much about their new domicile that he virtually ignores his kind grandfather (Richard Farnsworth) when he comes to visit. Steve Turner is dismayed when the development job goes bust. Lassie earns Matt's admiration when she drives off a wolf, quite a feat indeed, considering that Virginia is not known as a haven of wild wolves.

Matt and his sister start school at the tiny county school and find to their surprise that they like the other students and the teacher. The family has neighbor trouble from the wealthy faux cowboys of the Garland family on the enormous sheep farm next door. They have amassed their wealth partly from theft—they have been illegally using the Turners' farm to feed most of their animals for years. The old Collins farm, which Steve inherited from his deceased wife, has the richest pasturage in the county. Mr. Collins, the children's grandfather, moved and stopped maintaining it.

Matt and cute young neighbor April (Michelle Williams) team up to save a lamb lost in the woods. The eldest Garland son, Josh (Clayton Barclay Jones) also likes April. The Turners decide to go into sheep ranching, which incenses the elder Garland (Frederic Forrest). The two Garland boys drive their all-terrain vehicles perilously close to Turners' sheep. Lassie arrives and tears on their trouser cuffs — she takes her function as shepherd and guardian very seriously.

The head of the Garland clan decides to rustle themselves some sheep. He and his sons cut a piece of the fence and herd the entire Turner flock over to their place. Lassie is captured and escapes their shed via the window. Matt and Lassie are herding their sheep back home when Josh Garland emerges from the forest with his father's rifle, aiming it at the dog. Matt grabs the rifle from his hands and flings it into the nearby river. "That's my dad's best rifle!" Josh cries. He plunges in after it and nearly drowns. Matt goes in to save him and Steve Turner swims to them. Meanwhile, Lassie is caught by the current when trying to help Matt, and is swept away. Sam Garland and his sons are apologetic. Lassie still lives, miraculously, and she limps back to the schoolhouse for a reunion with Matt that comes straight from the pages of the original Eric Knight novel.

Lassie, 2005

The Dog Hero in Film

143

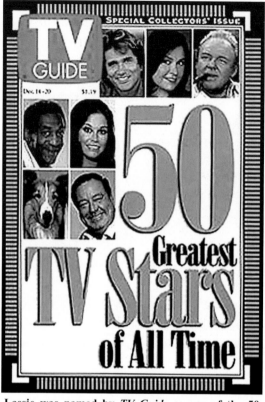

England's own version of *Lassie* is the latest retelling of the old Eric Knight story. Released in Europe in 2005 and in the U.S. in late 2006, the story tries to remain true to the old MGM version. There are a few variants. The unemployed Carracloughs (John Lynch and Samantha Morton) are persuaded by the Duke of Rudling (Peter O'Toole) to sell their purebred dog to him; while in the original Roddy McDowall version, they approach him with an offer. Joe (Jonathan Mason) is a bit younger than McDowall was when he played the role. From there the film resembles the earlier version quite closely.

Lassie was named by *TV Guide* as one of the 50 Greatest TV Stars of All Time.

Rowlie, played by the stout Edmund Gwenn in the MGM classic, is a little person, Peter Dinklage. A Pal descendant with the unlikely name of Mason portrays Lassie. Reviews have mostly been favorable. *The Associated Press'* Christy Lemire commented:

> Calling the film cathartic doesn't even begin to describe it.... Writer-director Charles Sturridge doesn't just tug on the heartstrings, he yanks at them relentlessly. But it's effective…and there's just something refreshingly quaint and classic about the Lassie stories, something so pure about the idea that the relationship between a boy and his dog can provide not just satisfying family entertainment, but a transforming moviegoing experience. That's especially true compared with the interchangeable animated films that come out each year.[5]

Neil Smith of the BBC wrote:

Lassie, the courageous collie with the heart of a lion and the navigational instincts of a homing pigeon, really does come home in Charles Sturridge's cosy family adventure, which brings the legendary mutt back across the Atlantic to the British setting of Eric Knight's original novel. Everything else adheres to feel-good Hollywood formula, though newcomers to the franchise may feel the same warm glow audiences felt 60 years ago when the eponymous pooch first barked on the silver screen.

When t' local pit closes, Yorkshire coal miner Sam Carraclough (John Lynch) and his stoic wife Sarah (Samantha Morton) have no option but to sell their son Joe's beloved bitch to the dotty Duke of Rudling (Peter O'Toole). Our hirsute heroine, however, has other ideas, foiling His Lordship's every attempt to keep her under lock and key.

"RAMBLING TRAVELOGUE"

When the Duke relocates to Scotland, it looks as if Joe (Jonathan Mason) will finally have to say farewell. Naturally Lassie thinks differently, beginning an arduous cross-country trek that sees her meet the Loch Ness monster, escape a Glasgow dog pound, testify in court and fall in with a traveling puppeteer (Peter Dinklage).

Episodic isn't the word for this rambling travelogue, in which a bewildering array of familiar faces (Edward Fox, Robert Hardy, Nicholas "Rodney" Lyndhurst) pop up for a succession of bizarrely brief cameos. Still, the combination of everyone's favourite canine and eye-catching Irish and Isle of Man locations ensure this nostalgic shaggy-dog story sends you home with your tail wagging.

CHAPTER SIX

THE DOG HERO
PURSUES A NEW IDENTITY

For the first few years of the 1970s, the American dog hero genre was at low ebb. The television series *Lassie* was cancelled after two decades on the air, and no studio was interested in a family friendly dog hero. This all changed with the release of *Benji* (1974). Benji is not the stereotypical dog hero, but nevertheless performs many of the heroic acts of a larger and more powerful dog. Part of his appeal lies in the fact that he does go against the stereotype. In addition, his character has the handicap of being a lap dog, one of the smaller breeds commonly regarded by fans of the working class of dogs as ineffectual creatures, useless animals that get underfoot and in the way. If large working dogs tend to be marginalized by human characters in a film's plot, a small lap dog is marginalized even further.

Benji must work even harder to get humans to help. *Benji* is a product of the 1970s, a time when films were breaking loose from the bonds of prior expectations. There had been a smattering of tiny-terrier heroes in decades past, such as Toto, who saved Dorothy from the Wicked Witch when she was in her clutches, but the public did not see Toto again until the Disney sequel of the 1980s, nor did Terry appear in any more heroic roles.

Benji had his beginning with the famed film of 1974, and continued his movie franchise with *For the Love of Benji* (1977) and *Benji the Hunted* (1987). This small reddish brown terrier mix only weighed about 15 pounds, but his films were heavyweights at the box office. His real name was Higgins and he had been a regular cast member of the mid-1960s television series *Petticoat Junction*. Producer and director Joe Camp wanted a film that returned the audience to a simpler form of moviemaking. *Benji* utilizes many shots with no dialogue, relying instead on the acting of the animals. The animal of the title is a semi-homeless dog that survives by doing adorable things like sitting up and begging for scraps of food. Benji lives in an abandoned mansion that has been locked up since the death of the old man who had once lived there. He enters it by means of a laborious walk up a garden wall and along a roof to a broken window on the second floor.

Among Benji's friends are two children, Cindy (Cynthia Smith) and Paul (Allen Fiuzat). Their doctor father (Peter Breck) is opposed to the idea of their handling germ-ridden strays, and banishes the dog from the house. Benji befriends another stray dog, a small white terrier his benefactors name Tiffany, and brings her along when he makes his rounds.

mulberry square productions present **Benji**

A family film by Joe Camp

GENERAL AUDIENCES

He has to rescue his two younger human friends when family friend Linda (Deborah Walley) uses their trust as a weapon. Her friends Riley (Tom Lester) and Mitch (Mark Slade) team up with Linda to make some quick money by kidnapping Paul and Cindy and hiding them in the old mansion. Benji sees the children in the mansion when he comes to eat some of the food the kidnappers have brought there. He realizes they are in trouble. Since no one is accustomed to taking a 15-pound dog seriously, Benji has difficulty when he goes for help. His first stop is the children's house. There, he sees three FBI agents examining a ransom note. A sudden flash of brilliance comes to him—if they like this piece of paper, they will follow him if he snatches it, and he can lead them to the house! The FBI agents are too quick for him. Benji, dejected, returns to the house and sees another chance to save the children. He grabs an earlier version of the ransom note actually given to the doctor, which is in a traceable handwriting. When he does so, they corner him and Tiffany bites one of them. Mitch kicks her and Benji sees her still form in a heap in a corner. In a plot device that could have been taken from a yellowed old Rin-Tin-Tin movie script, Benji must make a decision: stay and defend his mate or take the note

to the humans who might be able to help them. He returns to the home of the children and sees one of the kidnappers visiting at the doctor's home under the very noses of FBI agents! "Nice doggie, come here, doggie," Linda coos to the distrustful dog to get within a foot or so of him, and the ransom note goes directly from his mouth to her purse. The housekeeper (Patsy Garrett) scolds him, "Oh, Benji, come here, and stop bothering these busy people!" She picks him up and starts to carry him away. Benji bites the portly woman and she drops him. "He bit me!" she cries, more out of surprise than pain. "I told you that stray dogs are nothing but trouble," the children's father admonishes her. Benji takes advantage of the confusion to grab the purse. The FBI agents see the note fall out of Linda's purse and she confesses. Audience members familiar with dog behavior would at once notice the discrepancy between the kind of shelter-seeking behavior shown by the lead canine character and that shown by real dogs. When looking for shelter, dogs burrow into the soil or nest in thick hedges beneath piles of pine needles and leaves; they do not climb up onto ledges and rooftops. Benji's ability to understand that the piece of paper in Linda's handbag will enable the FBI to help him is beyond the mental prowess of any dog. The audiences did not mind; they came to the theaters en masse to the delight of the producers. *The New York Times* grudgingly gave good marks to the film:

> Cynophobes are warned...that Benji, a diminutive, bright-eyed, brown, shaggy bundle of energy and a veteran of movies and television, most notably this '*Petticoat Junction*' series, dominates his human supporting players. If Benji, like his rudimentary story, is improbable, he's a good deal more lovable than Cynthia Smith and Allen Fiuzat, as the kids who adore him; Patsy Garrett, as their understanding housekeeper; Peter Breck, as their father, and Deborah Walley, Tom Lester, and Mark Slade, as the somewhat silly, callow kidnappers.[1]

"Practically perfect... bright, funny, inventive!"
Les Angeles Times

According to *Variety*, *Benji* was the number three moneymaker for the year 1974, just behind *The Towering Inferno*. The title theme for the original film won the Golden Globe that year and was nominated for an Academy Award. The American Guild of Variety Artists' Animal Entertainer of the Year Award was twice awarded to Higgins. *Underdog*, a book about his journey from an animal shelter to the Golden Globe Awards, was a popular seller. *Benji, Benji's Very Own Christmas Story* (1978) and *Benji Takes a Dive at Marineland* (1981) are available on home video. More significantly, the film reduced prejudices against non-pedigreed dogs, and increased adoptions from animal shelters all over the United States. This is evidenced by the American Humane's press release of the late 1990s stating that because Higgins, the canine actor, was adopted from a shelter, public attitudes toward shelters have improved substantially. In addition, his owner and trainer has partnered with Pets911.com, an adoption service for dogs that are in dire need of homes.[2]

Frank Inn, Higgins' trainer, achieved worldwide fame. Inn actually had many decades of experience in training animals for motion pictures and had learned the trade from Jack Weatherwax as long ago as the late 1930s, having assisted him in training the Cairn Terrier in *The Wizard of Oz* (1939).[3]

Oh Heavenly Dog! (1980) was a *Benji* sequel starring Chevy Chase as a detective named Browning. It departed from the dog hero tradition and moves into fantasy, becoming a sort of doggie version of *Here Comes Mr. Jordan.*

Benji and Lizard Paw are the best of doggie friends in *Benji: Off the Leash!*

The film made a profit, but the *Benji* sequels ceased for two decades. The Benji character was to return in 2004 with *Benji: Off the Leash!* The tagline of the film was "Rules are made to be housebroken." In his Sun Times 2004 review, film critic Roger Ebert said, *"Benji: Off the Leash* is not one of the great dog movies,

Baby in *Benji: Off the Leash!*

but it's a good one, abandoning wall-to-wall cuteness for a drama about a homeless puppy. And it sends a valuable message: Mongrels are just as lovable as pure breeds, or maybe in the case of Benji and Shaggy, the stars of this film, more so." The film won the Genesis Award in 2005 for Family Feature Film.

The total retail gross for all Benji products, including the films and the

television specials, is approximately 230 million dollars.[4]

Italian director Lucio Fulci, mainly known for his ultra-violent bloodfest films, directed his first and only dog hero film, *White Fang* (*Zanna Bianca*), in 1973. The film boasted a major international cast including Franco Nero as Jason Scott, Virna Lisi as Sister Evangelina and Fernando Rey as Father Oatley. The film picks up where *Call of the Wild* ends. White Fang is the son of Buck from *Call of the Wild.* An Eskimo boy Mitsah (Missaele) finds both dogs. Buck soon dies and his family adopt White Fang. The film goes back and forth between the good guys and the bad guys, good winning in the end. As per his reputation, Fulci does have two brutal fight scenes between White Fang and another dog and then a bear. *Variety* (1/1/90) remarked it was, "an excellent remake." Tonino Ricci directed its sequel, *White Fang To the Rescue* (*Zanna Bianca alla Riscossa*), in 1974. Italian cinema has very seldom explored the dog hero genre, and these are among the very rare examples.

Bearheart starred in *Legend of the Northwest* (1978), which is also known as *Legend of Bearheart*, (the film is available for sale under that title). Film Foundry Partners, producers of the comedy *Summer-dog* (1977), produced this 1978 film. Set in a town called Babylon, Oregon, in the late 1880s, *Legend of the Northwest* begins with the usual widower and his son and daughter who are starting a new life in a new town. They purchase a trading post and are setting up housekeeping when a wild dog arrives to drive off a bear and save the daughter. The father injures the dog, thinking it to be dangerous. A trapper named Abe (Denver Pyle, often cast in this sort of film) helps the family treat the dog's injury. He shares with them the local legend of Bearheart, a noble dog who drove the cold-blooded killer of his owner, the

Bearheart

manager of the local trading post, to a state of insanity. The killer sought the help of the local sheriff against the German Shepherd dog that stayed just out of range of his bullets, denied him food and water and kept him up all night with his howls. Bearheart developed a hatred of rifles. It was a rifle that the villain used to beat him unconscious, and then kill his beloved master. The dog's paranoid fear of rifles provokes a response when a little boy in the town brandishes one as he walks down the dusty street of the Old West town. Bearheart knocks the boy down and, from the filmgoer's viewpoint, appears to be mauling him. It is all a misunderstanding; the dog was merely trying to get the dangerous rifle away from the boy. At the end of the film, this symbol of raw vengeance loses all desire to be violent, and resumes the life of a domestic dog with his new family.

Legend of the Northwest pilfered many plot lines from *The Painted Hills*, which had been released over 20 years earlier; however, *Legend of the Northwest* was largely ignored by critics and the general public, so this borrowing was hardly noticed.

The early 1980s marked the end of another dog hero cycle in film. The time was not ripe for cinematic dog heroes to make a return to the silver screen or money for their masters until the very end of that decade, when the next

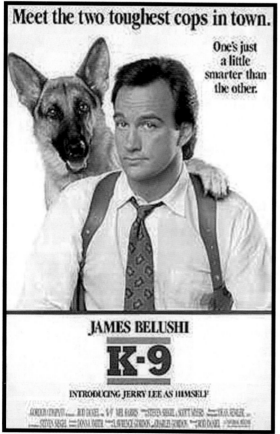

dog hero cycle boomed with Jerry Lee in *K-9* (1989) and Beasley in *Turner and Hooch* (1989), both very popular and very similar to one another.

K-9 is partly a comedy and partly a serious drama. The film uses the popular cinematic convention of an erratic, loose cannon cop teamed with another cop as part of some sort of rehabilitation forced upon him by his Chief. Of course the two antagonistic partners become friends after one risks his life for the other. The only difference in this film is that one of the partners is the dog Jerry Lee. James Belushi is the stressed out Thomas Dooley,

Jerry Lee in *K-9*

who asks for a dog as his partner because he can't stand any of the human officers he has been assigned. Initially he holds the quirky dog in contempt—the dog helps himself to Dooley's bed while Dooley and his girlfriend are in it. Dooley decides to keep the beast amused for a few hours by giving him a completely frozen steak from the freezer. Jerry Lee eats it in 10 seconds flat. "All right, let's get one thing straight: The woman is mine!" he tells the animal in a private conference, and continues:

> Now we're both members of the animal kingdom. You know
> that and I know that. And we both know that this thing is really
> primal. So if you think you're such a badass you just try that
> one more time and you're gonna end up in a pet cemetery! You
> remember the movie *Old Yeller*? You remember when they shot
> him in the end? I didn't cry!

Dooley's attitude toward Jerry Lee changes when the dog sniffs out a cop killer and leads him to a well-groomed kingpin of the San Diego drug trade, Ken Lyman (Kevin Tighe). The drug lord has Dooley's girlfriend Tracy (Mel Harris) kidnapped and is holding her as a way to keep him from stopping a major drug shipment. In a tense scene, Dooley arrives at a predetermined drop point where Lyman is about to airlift a car transport that contains millions of dollars

Jim Belushi as Dooley with Jerry Lee in *K-9*

of cocaine. Dooley commandeers it, holds Lyman off with a phony bomb timer, and with the help of his partner, stops Lyman's henchmen. The kingpin flees, shooting Jerry. Seeing this, Dooley fires about 10 bullets into him. He then rushes the dog to a regular hospital, the only one he can find quickly.

Dooley thinks the dog had died. "I know we didn't exactly click as partners and the way it looks now, we never will," he says aloud. The dog is quite alive, only lying very quietly in the recovery room. "I shouldn't have yelled at you. I yelled a lot. I know it could have been partially my fault. I put you through a car wash. That was not a good thing to do. I yelled at you because you broke my Mustang's side view mirror. That was a vintage Mustang but…I shouldn't have yelled at you. If you were around right now, we'd go to Vegas. We could pick up that poodle at the beach. She was hot! You could even sleep on the bed…at the foot." Jerry opens one eye. Annoyed at Jerry for pretending to be a goner, Dooley yells, "You asshole! Were you listening to everything I said? Because I thought I was talking to a dead dog."

Dooley makes good his promise to take the girlfriends, both human and canine, with them to Las Vegas. Stephen Holden, *The New York Times'* reviewer, wrote, "*K-9* doesn't have a shred of credibility. And Mr. Belushi, despite some rough edges, lacks a strong enough macho growl to make Dooley seem like a police dog in human clothing. *K-9* is at least mildly diverting. If the movie has any success, one can envisage many barking, yapping sequels to come."[5] His prediction proved accurate. Two sequels, *K-911* (1999) and *K-9: P. I.* (2002) were sold as direct to video releases.

Bingo appeared in theaters in 1991. Bingo, a yellow collie mix, works for a circus dog trainer who expects him to fill in for a temporarily sidelined poodle star who has stepped on a nail. The act the dog is supposed to perform involves jumping though a flaming hoop before a live audience. Bingo, smarter than his master, refuses. The trainer goes into a rage after the act, and grabs his pistol. "I'm shooting that worthless mutt!" he shouts. Bingo flees and ,while wandering in the woods, encounters a boy named Chuckie Devlin (Robert J. Steinmiller). Bingo applies artificial resuscitation to save the boy when he nearly drowns, neatly hangs his wet clothes on a makeshift clothesline in the woods and uses a fresh fish to distract a bear so they can climb a tree to escape.

Chuckie returns home the following morning after the bear leaves, and his father (David Rasche) instructs his mother (Cindy Williams) to pretend not to care that he was missing all night. This is his father's way of teaching him a lesson. Chuckie hides Bingo in his room. His father, a kicker for the Denver Broncos, is traded to another team. The family moves and Bingo follows. The family stops at Duke's Truck Stop for some "good old American fare." Chuckie accidentally stumbles upon cages out back with dogs in them, and a butcher making hot dogs. "We make 'em fresh!" brags the butcher. Chuckie tells his parents. "So?" his father responds. Bingo is captured and tossed into a cage. He

rescues the other canines, and continues to follow the Devlin family. On the way he foils a pair of criminals who abduct Chuckie for ransom and try to kill Bingo and Chuckie by blowing up a warehouse. The brave little dog is injured but recovers in a hospital surrounded by the Devlin family. With the family are assorted individuals who wanted only to do him bodily harm earlier in the picture. *Bingo* slyly winks at the audience as it spoofs dog hero conventions, going far beyond the typical canine exploits seen *Lassie*: Bingo romances a neighborhood Cocker Spaniel female with flowers and a bottle of champagne; Bingo pitches a pup tent; Bingo disposes of the hot dog manufacturing plant by tying up the butcher and his family and driving their pickup truck into the building.

In classic dog hero films the human recipients of bow-wow benevolence are all good people. Chuckie and Chickie are decent people; however, the parents are banal, obnoxious and self-centered—aka perfect fodder for satires of American suburbia. The children could well be the clichéd orphans of older dog hero films. Their parents long ago emotionally abandoned their children. Devlin Senior's football-worshipping wife does not take him to task for staying on the field while vicious criminals abduct one of his sons. In fact, Chuckie's mother has to listen to the game's progress on the deputy sheriff's radio as she rides with him to the warehouse.

The producers appear to have made a bad error in judgment when they used strong language in the film, since children were the demographic sought by the advertising and promotion departments. Both child and adult characters use four letter words and rude hand gestures. PG-13 language and situations occur frequently, thus not endearing the picture to parents. The film cost $10 million and earned $8 million in box-office receipts. The dog hero genre is still awaiting a quality spoof viewable by families.

An unusually realistic film for Disney, *White Fang* (1991) features the adventures of a teenage boy named Jack Conroy (Ethan Hawke), modeled after Jack London, the author of the original novel. Jack journeys to Alaska during the Gold Rush days to claim his father's cabin and continue working his claim with his father's partner, Alex Larson (Klaus Maria Brandauer). Alaska is so raw and the humans so dangerous that one wonders if the boy will make it out alive with the money he brought with him. Jack proves himself strong enough and smart enough to survive. Dutch (Seymour Cassel) is at first very reluctant to  have Jack along. Their first task, before they even reach the cabin, is to bury the frozen corpse of Alex's and Dutch's recently deceased partner in a remote spot where they had promised to lay him to rest. They must abandon the plan when the corpse and the sled that carries it slide down a slope into an icy lake.

White Fang

One night wolves prowl the camp for food and find it by luring away a sled dog. Dutch searches for the dog alone and is killed. The two surviving humans and their dogs make it to a trading post where Jack meets a wolf hybrid (played by Jed) belonging to a Native American. The dog saves Jack from a bear and the two become allies. The animal's owner is blackmailed into selling White Fang, as he calls him, to a cruel dog fighter, Beauty Smith (James Remar). An officer, who breaks up Smith's dog fighting trade, presents White Fang to Jack. Jack, Alex and the wolf dog move to the cabin near Jack's father's claim, and Jack begins teaching White Fang to trust him. White Fang symbolizes the raw and wild land, which becomes welcoming when one approaches the land with respect. Hostility is more of an anthropomorphic attribute that humans assign to a landscape than it is an actual feature in *White Fang*.

Jack teaches Alex to read and write, and the claim starts to pay off at last. This fact is not lost on the cruel dog fighter, who sets fire to the cabin and plans to kill Jack, Alex and White Fang. The trio outwits him and keep the cabin and claim.

The perhaps the inevitable sequel followed. *White Fang 2: Myth of the White Wolf* (Disney, 1994) shifted its focus away from Jack and toward his friend Henry Casey (Scott Bairstow). Henry and White Fang have been working Jack's mine while he is away building a hotel.

A short distance away, the Haida tribe is in trouble. The caribou herd has not returned from migration. If they do not return the people will starve. The local minister, Reverend Drury (Al Molina) is pressuring the people to leave.

The tribe's chief, Moses Joseph (Al Harrington), has a dream about a white wolf emerging from a stream and his lovely niece Lily (Charmaine Craig) going to meet it. He awakens her and tells her that this means that she must go out to seek the white wolf, the restorer of the caribou. He advises that this white wolf may be a shape shifter.

Meanwhile, Henry encounters a stranger after Henry's gold who tries to shoot him and trap White Fang. Rushing the gold to market, Henry rides a raft down a swollen river. The raft capsizes and the two are almost killed. Lily sees the wolf disappear beneath the waves as the man appears, and deduces that the man is the white wolf and rescues him. Henry is welcomed to the village as their hero, but he is more worried about his missing dog and gold.

Scott Bairstow and Charmaine Craig with Jed in *White Fang 2*

Henry cannot convince the Haidas that he is not the one who will bring back the caribou. He cannot even purchase food for them on credit. Discouraged, Henry prepares to leave. "I sang the healing song for you. I gave you back your life!" Lily fumes. "All you care about is your gold!"

"I'm grateful. But I'm not going to some God-forsaken place to hunt caribou!"

"You are just like every other white man," Lily says, turning away from him. Lily's brother Peter (Anthony Ruivivar) befriends him and teaches him archery. He jokingly tells Henry that he plans to come back after death as a raven to caw all night and keep people up. A strange encounter with Reverend Drury turns hostile after Henry politely turns down an extremely well-paying job he offers because Henry must help the tribe. Henry is also sure that this man is not a real minister.

Henry dreams of a white wolf and, when he tells Lily's great uncle, they are all convinced that he is the one who will help them. White Fang is reunited with Henry, and then he and Lily's brother enter the wilderness to search for the caribou. While hunting, someone tries to kill them. Peter falls and disappears in the shrubbery and Henry is swung up into the trees via a rope trap.

Lily has followed them and cuts Henry down. The two discover what has happened to the caribou—someone has built a rock wall and the animals huddle

AN ANCIENT MYTH. A LAND OF MYSTERY.
AN EXTRAORDINARY ADVENTURE.

WHITE FANG 2
MYTH OF THE WHITE WOLF

near it, their instincts drawing them toward the grazing lands on the other side.

The two fall down a mine shaft. Who do they encounter in the mine?—the man who shot the brother and the phony Reverend who are forcing Indians at gunpoint to work the unauthorized mine. Lily and Henry escape, grab some dynamite and head toward the rock wall. Peter reappears safe and sound and leads them away from the mine. White Fang loses them but an unusually tame raven shows him the way. Lily and Henry blow an opening in the rock wall but then Drury captures Lily and tries to escape. White Fang and Henry leap on him, serial style, from an outcropping along the road. Henry unties Lily and the three jump off just before the wagon tumbles into a canyon.

Henry, Lily and the liberated Haidas return to find Peter lying dead—his back was broken when he was shot. "This is impossible!" Henry exclaims, dumbfounded.

The film ends depicting Lily, Moses Joseph, Henry, a white female wolf and the proud White Fang with a litter of pups in the old Rin-Tin-Tin tradition. He is not quite the patriarch Rin-Tin-Tin was, however, because he only has *five* pups instead of Rinty's usual six or seven. *White Fang II: Myth of the White Wolf* has every B-movie dog hero convention that could be resuscitated: noble indigenous people with mystical powers, daring stunts, a brave dog, a pretty girl and villains trying to kill a miner and kidnap the heroine. Thank goodness the Disney screenwriters did not forget the mate and the cute puppies in the closing shot.

A Quebec film company, Blue Rider Pictures, faithfully brought another Jack London novel to life for television in 1997. Three dogs, Gustave, Gessa and Vosko, were used to portray Buck in *The Call of the Wild: Dog of the Yukon.* The film followed the life of a Saint Bernard named Buck, who is stolen from his San Francisco family during the late 1890s and sold to a postal courier in the Yukon. Here, strong dogs with heavy fur coats are almost as valuable as gold. The only conveyance that works in the frigid Alaskan gold country is the dogsled. Thus, every large furry dog along the entire West Coast is coveted, an historical fact of the Gold Rush days.

Buck learns to be ruthless and cunning to survive. At their first stop their driver, the postal courier, has an emergency assignment. Reluctantly, he sells the dog team to a young man from back East who, along with his wife, his brother and several of her family members, is beginning his journey of prospecting for gold in the mountains. They promise to rest the dogs for a week. As soon as the postal courier is out of sight, they strike off for the wilderness. Clueless about the ways of the North, they almost run out of food after one day. Team leader Buck balks when driven toward a frozen lake, and the young wife's brother threatens to kill the dog for defying him. The husband's brother, John Thornton, stands between them and says it is his brother's dog. "Leave him alone. Something is wrong and he knows it!" Thornton warns him. They leave Thornton and Buck on the shore and set off across the lake. The ice cracks and the entire party falls into the water and perish.

The huge dog regains some faith in the human species when he learns to trust the sensible, kind prospector. Buck is raw animal vitality, and his

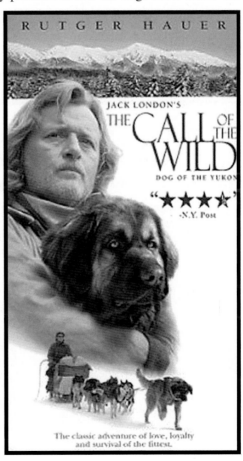

RUTGER HAUER

JACK LONDON'S

THE CALL OF THE WILD

DOG OF THE YUKON

"★★★★"
-N.Y. Post

The classic adventure of love, loyalty and survival of the fittest.

love is a fierce sort of love—the pure love of a dog that will make it choose a human benefactor over a female. Thornton finally strikes gold, only to be killed by a claim jumper. Buck kills the murderer and flees into the forest where he lives among the wolves and becomes a legend among the Native Americans. The film is brutally realistic in many ways, and depicts (simulated) animal and human suffering and death. The film was not a major success among viewers despite Richard Dreyfuss' well-done narration and the acting talents of Rutger Hauer as John Thornton. The music was unusually lush for a made-for-television film of this genre and was performed by the Peymeinode Symphony Orchestra.

The question is whether such a film depicting the darker side of human and animal nature trivializes animal-to-animal and human-to-animal violence or emphasizes the need for improvement. This author maintains that such a film, intelligently showing both the good and the bad in animal/human relationships, has a greater ability to increase consciousness of the difficulties animals face than does the family friendly *Beethoven* (1992). *The New York Times* critic Janet Maslin praised Beethoven because of "a cute pet, a squeaky-clean family and quaintly harmless notions of villainy."[6]

Beethoven depicts the life of another Saint Bernard, this one is the pampered dog of a suburban family.

His sloppy and mischievous habits threaten him with expulsion from the family unit. We, the audience, know already that a handsome middle-class family in such a comedy would never consider dumping a dog off on a lonely stretch of rural highway or take him to the pound to get rid of him. Beethoven saves young Emily Newton (Sara Rose Karr) from drowning, and even if he had not performed this heroic act to secure his own future, we know that the story will have a happy conclusion and that the disgruntled but kind George Newton (Charles Grodin) will see the error of his ways and save the dog. However, any viewer of this film who is aware of the social problem of pet abandonment knows that in the real world middle class and even wealthy families abandon dogs, and it is not something limited to impoverished families.

A second aspect of the plot bears discussion. In *Beethoven*, the title dog escapes an evil veterinarian, Dr. Varnick (Dean Jones), to come to live with the Newtons. Dr. Varnick wants Beethoven for experiments. He smears red dye on his clothes to make it appear Beethoven attacked him. He can then pretend to put him to sleep and use him for the experiments.

Unethical veterinarians do exist, but their misdeeds are likely to be far different from those depicted in *Beethoven* such as cover-ups of malpractice or dumping unhealthy animals they have bred on the doorsteps of animal shelters. The public's love of animals has made such veterinarians the subject of news stories and media investigations. Furthermore, general practice veterinarians are not in the business of researching exploding bullets. Anyone wanting to obtain live dogs for nefarious reasons need only telephone a puppy mill or comb the classified advertisements of most newspapers to obtain dogs listed as "free to a good home."

But reality does not really enter into a family-friendly puppy tale. It's true that viewers will have a good time watching a popcorn flick, but the audience will learn nothing about the reality of animal experimentation—a dark and fantastic subject that is the subject of several excellent documentaries.

CHAPTER SEVEN

THE DOG HERO FILM
AND PUBLIC PERCEPTION,
VALUES AND ETHICS

The use of domestic and wild animals in filmmaking naturally has raised ethical questions. In the earliest decades of world cinema, motion picture crews sometimes caused the deaths of animals, either accidentally or purposely. In his book *Animals in Film*, Jonathan Burt cited an interview with Rob Block, owner of the modern training company Critters of the Cinema. Originally, said Block, the animal entertainment industry attracted the sort of person who had no problem with killing an animal if it meant a successful shot. When possible, the directors and animal wranglers of the 1920s would provide rubber covers for teeth and claws during fight scenes. They usually used dummy dogs in long shots when the scene called for dogs to be shot. However, if such a feat were not feasible, real animals were used. Only the most recognizable animal stars received any special consideration. When a non-famous animal performer or stunt animal died, who would ever know? Such information did not make it to

Even in the 1920s, studios had the power to hush up unpleasant stories such as the deaths during *Noah's Ark*.

the pages of the consumer magazines. On rare occasions, information about the death of an acting animal was leaked but usually only when a human death occurred at the same time. In 1928, such an event reached scandalous proportions when during the filming of Warner Bros.' *Noah's Ark* three extras died during the film's epic flood scene. The extras had not been warned of the force of the water when the floodgates were opened on the outdoor set. In addition to the extras, several donkeys also drowned, and a dozen people were injured.

It was during the 1930s that Britain took the lead in the Western world with the passage of the Cinematograph Films (Animal) Act of 1937. Protection for film animals came to the United States a few years later, in 1940. Although the Hays Office enforcement of the Production Code Administration's rules was excessive and often ridiculous in censoring content and presentation in films produced between 1932 and 1966, it did, however, have its positive side. The American Humane Association and the Society for the Prevention of Cruelty to Animals joined forces with the Hays Office to provide some protection for animals on movie sets. Up to that time, animal deaths had been a common occurrence in motion pictures. Though most animal deaths and injuries depicted onscreen were simulated with dummies, rubber teeth, rubber hooves and clever editing, it was not possible at that time to know for certain if any animals were injured or killed during the filming—and producers and press agents were not likely to admit to animal abuse or endangerment. The proverbial straw that broke the camel's back was the film *Jesse James*, released in 1939 by 20th Century Fox. Filmed mostly on location in a small town in Missouri, the film featured a scene of a horse being ridden off a 70-foot cliff into water. The animal died, and the public and industry outcry was considerable. Therefore, beginning in

Stunt over a cliff in *Jesse James* that killed the horse.

the 1940s, the Hays Office arranged for humane workers to be present during filming to protect the welfare of animals. Abuse like tripping livestock with wire rigs known as the "Running W" was once standard practice.[1] Happily, the Production Code Administration forbade this and later, the American Humane Association reinforced the Code.

The Patsy (Picture Animal Top Star of the Year) Awards were a staple in the 1950s through the 1970s, and animal actors regularly received them until several years ago. Francis the Talking Mule received the first such award. The focus of the awards was humane treatment and training methods for film animals. Francis the Mule actually shared honors with her trainers.

Enforcement of protections waned for a time after 1966 with the closing of the Hays Office. Unbelievably, the old ways of tripping cows and horses returned in a few pictures. The first year that the AHA was able to have a clause inserted into the contract of every motion picture involving animals was 1977. This gave some measure of control to the American Humane Association over the screenplay itself. One of the new powers it gained was the ability to determine how many hours an individual animal could be worked per day.

The AHA generally has a very tiny staff and no more than approximately nine field personnel, making the daily supervision of every film impossible. Filming takes place year round in Southern California, and almost year round in other states. Daily monitoring is not possible on each film using an animal. Consequently, self-regulation by the film industry is a must for animals to be truly provided humane and safe working conditions. A plethora of companies devoted exclusively to the training of animals for motion pictures, advertisements and television programs have cropped up in the last two decades. They mostly belong to the Animal Consultants and Trainers Association, founded in 1989.[2]

Hollywood's obsession with trends and fads—specifically animal-related ones—raises ethical questions. Breed fads are a byproduct of successful

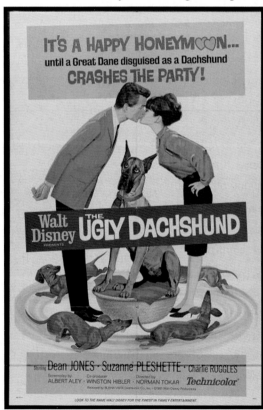

IT'S A HAPPY HONEYMOON...
until a Great Dane disguised as a Dachshund
CRASHES THE PARTY!

Walt Disney PRESENTS THE UGLY DACHSHUND

Starring Dean JONES · Suzanne PLESHETTE · Charlie RUGGLES
Screenplay by ALBERT ALEY · Co-producer WINSTON HIBLER · Directed by NORMAN TOKAR · Technicolor

motion pictures and television programs. The almost manic desire to appear hip and popular perpetuates a desire to possess items seen in the possession of celebrities or in movies and on television. Many people in Western culture regard animals as property, although as more and more animals become valued family members, humans are calling for new legal and ethical definitions of animals. Meantime, the concept of a pet as something to help a person stay fashionable and up to date still persists. While trendy fads come and go, a dog has a lifespan lasting far longer than the dura-

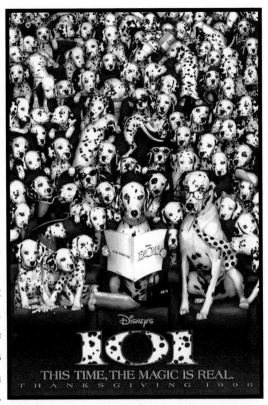

tion of a new craze. It's not only celebrities toting around pocketbook dogs who are to blame. Often because of a film's huge box-office success, breeders will mass-produce the breed that had been featured in the film. Problems often ensue when the breed has special requirements that do not work well with every household. A case in point was the Dalmatian, a very active working breed made popular by the Disney film *101 Dalmatians* (1996) and its sequels as

well as the immense popularity of the Taco Bell Chihuahua. Responsibility lies with pet owners who do not educate themselves about the breeds they choose to buy, the filmmakers, whose greed overrides ethics, and unconcerned dog breeders whose bottom line is profit.

Lassie poses for publicity photos in 1958.

Let's face it, animals are either adorable or frightening and will always make good movie material. And it is unreasonable to eliminate all animals from films out of concern that a fad may result — especially dogs, which are, paws down, the most popular. A reasonable approach to the problem is to make the argument that filmmakers owe it to the animals to be more responsible toward both them and their owners. Film is a powerful medium and there really are audience members who use wishful thinking rather than critical thinking and will acquire a pet because it is trendy. These are the audience members whom filmmakers could consider when producing a motion picture starring an animal. A crafty Bloodhound in a film will not necessarily make millions rush to breeders and order one. However, if the film portrayed Bloodhounds as the best dogs for everyone because of their extreme adaptability and their incredible athleticism and the slapstick humor that results from owning one — well, the filmmakers would be purposely misrepresenting the breed. Thousands would be entranced by the film and would create a demand for a Bloodhound — a basically overlooked breed. It is regrettable knowing that thousands of people who purchased purebred collies over the years thought they were getting Lassie, only to be disappointed when their dogs did not find any kid down a well or spent their days catching crooks but wound up with a real dog that had accidents on the rug, ate your shoes and preferred catching mice and rabbits to crooks.

While it is true that canine heroes abound in real life, they are not limited to any particular breed. Furthermore, not every companion animal is going to behave like the Benji hero commonly found in the world of entertainment. Nor will every companion animal be a Beethoven–type, whose disorderly behavior would work through an unsuspecting household into chaos. This is fortunate indeed, as most of us would much prefer the mannerly Benji. But really, in the end people themselves must take responsibility in realizing that a dog is a huge commitment and not something to be selected because of a movie-induced dog fad. A knowledgeable public, willing to discard fantasy and look realistically at motion picture production, will reduce the problem of breed fads. Filmgoers can educate one another about the difference between a dog actor on screen and a frisky real-life dog. People must learn that these characters' unusual exploits and appearances result from a combination of training, genuine acting skills on the part of the dog, as well as the work of the cinematographer, special effects department and film editor. And just like people, living dog heroes can come in all shapes, sizes and colors.

THE DOG HERO ON THE BORDER WHERE THE FUTURE BEGINS

Above: *White Fang,* **1991**
Below: Kelsey Grammer and Moose from *Frasier*

Today dog hero actors in modern films have little name recognition. Few people who saw *White Fang* could even name the animal star, or even the name of the little dog in the television comedy *Frasier*, a show that was seen week after week. With the exception of *Benji* and its sequels, the animal's name is no longer on the marquee. In today's world, a computer-generated dog created by a team of 30 CGI experts is often as popular as a real animal that spends weeks or months becoming physically and psychologically readied for its role.

Computer games provide entertainment and vicarious action, but even the most hardcore gaming and CGI film fan will shut off the machine for a time and seek something more real. Many of us want to feel a cold nose attached to a warm and loving furry canine friend. A cuddly pal that can show nobility, intelligence, bravery and unconditional love is a rare gift.

Moreover, that connectedness to the mind and spirit of a living dog is something most of humanity does not want to do without. Dog lovers want to see reminders of some marvelous creature they know or have known. They go to the movies or watch television so that this connection to nature and life can be relived by watching the exploits of a two-dimen-

Maya from *Eight Below*

sional cinematic dog onscreen. Early filmgoers looked for this connection in 1921 in *The Silent Call,* and today's audiences find it in films like *Eight Below* as well as the classics available on DVD.

As they say, everything old is new again, and the cycle of dog hero films is no exception. The new films include *Benji: Off The Leash!*, which was released in the fall of 2004. This new Benji story was the first in over 20 years. The original Higgins who played Benji, of course, is long dead, and his original director and screenwriter Joe Camp adopted a female terrier mix slightly resembling Higgins from a Mississippi animal shelter.[1] In this sequel Benji has been bred in a puppy mill. Unscrupulous breeder Hatchett (Chris Kendrick) breeds Benji's mother as many times per year as her body can endure. Hatchett is very disappointed with the results of her latest litter and throws the poor little pups into a bag and drops it in the forest. His young son Colby (Nick Whitaker) rescues them and takes them to an abandoned house. Colby knows how important it is to nourish the tiny pups and brings their mother over once a day to nurse them. One of her offspring is a little fluffy blond dog that Nick has named Puppy—soon to be the future Benji. Unfortunately, Hatchett discovers the puppies and forbids Nick to feed them. Nick hides Benji in his private clubhouse in the woods and the pup grows up in this refuge, secretly nursed by his mother until he is old enough to eat solid food.

The Hatchett family is a model of dysfunction. The father scarcely speaks to either his wife or his child unless it is to bark orders at them or tell them how

The Dog Hero in Film

Benji opens a cage in *Benji: Off the Leash*!

disappointed he is in their behavior. Benji runs away when Hatchett discovers the hidden clubhouse and forms a pack with a mongrel named Lizard Tongue. Benji is determined to rescue his mother, and his old friend Colby (Nick Whitaker) lets them get away on their second attempt.

Lizard Tongue and Benji have comical scrapes with two dogcatchers who chase Benji to the old house where he had hidden his mother who is very ill and weak. The dogcatchers take them to a shelter and the kind animal control administrator tries to telephone Hatchett to tell him that one of his breeding females has a severe uterine infection and needs emergency surgery that will render her unable to have any more pups. Failing to get permission, she decides to go ahead with the operation.

A Hollywood talent scout sees newspaper stories about the little dog's heroism. The talent scout conspires with the local police and the animal control officer to catch Hatchett, who has managed always to stay just a few steps ahead of the law. The regional newspaper carries the exciting news that a local dog hero has been selected to be in the movies.

Hatchett recognizes "his" dog Benji in the newspaper and the greedy villain shows up at the animal control office to claim his dog and meet the talent scout. "This is your dog?" he is asked. "Yes. I bred him," Hatchett replies.

Benji: Off the Leash!

The officer motions toward Benji's mother, "Then this dog must be your dog too." "Yes," he asserts. "You're under arrest for animal cruelty," she tells him. Colby has finally convinced Mrs. Hatchett to admit to the authorities that her husband abused her.

In the final shots, Benji and Lizard Tongue reenact their brave deeds for the motion picture cameras in locales identical to those in the film that we have just seen. The animal action is also identical. The film leaves audiences wondering what was the significance of this movie within a movie? Was the story of Benji just another movie for the fictitious filmmakers, or did they use events from Benji's real life as a basis for the film they came to the little town to produce? *Variety*'s Joe Leydon explains the opening and closing quasi-documentary bits as: "Modestly clever framing device indicates *Off the Leash* provides back story of latest canine to be cast as Benji."

Benji begins the film as a very timid dog. When he sees how ill his mother is and how Colby suffers just because he is helping, he takes action and overcomes his fear. After two attempts, he manages to free his mother and take her to the old house he remembers from his puppy days. Lizard Tongue and Benji form an odd kind of relationship with the dogcatchers and Benji goes to them for help. Colby's bravery then rubs off on his mother and they all take steps to end Hatchett's reign of terror.

Bruce Greenwood and Maya in *Eight Below*

Eight Below was released by Disney in February 2006 and was a box-office hit—its opening weekend grossed over $24 million with a worldwide gross of over $106 million. The film is a remake of the Japanese film *Nankyoku Monogatari* (1983). It was based on a true story from 1957 when a dog team was left behind at a scientific outpost in Antarctica; two dogs survived to be reunited with their human companions and were honored as heroes back in Japan.

Eight Below stars Paul Walker as Jerry Shepherd, a member of a team maintaining a scientific research station in Antarctica in the early 1990s. He and his friend and colleague, Charlie Cooper (Jason Biggs), assist a scientist, Davis McClaren (Bruce Greenwood), who has journeyed to this desolate continent to search for a meteorite from the collision of a small cosmic body with the planet Mercury. Jerry and Dr. McClaren set forth via dogsled to where the scientist believes the meteorites may have fallen. It is January, the middle of summer, and the going is treacherous because of melting ice. Blizzards still occur even in summer, and the base radios to them that a storm is on the way. Static on the radio prevents them from hearing when the storm is expected. Not wishing to disappoint McClaren, Jerry allows him a few more hours to search before they start back. He finds a meteorite and slips on the ice, nearly falling into a lake. Maya, Jerry's favorite dog, saves him by placing a rope over McClaren's head and arm and pulling him from the freezing water. They have to make their way back to the base through the storm while injured—Jerry with frostbitten hands despite his gloves. They are airlifted to an Antarctic field hospital. Katie (Moon Bloodgood), the pilot and Jerry's former lover, promises that they will return for the eight Huskies and Malamutes, but the storm intensifies and the Navy

Maya, Max and Buck in *Eight Below*

cannot help; all ships are being deployed back to New Zealand. Katie tells him she is sorry she cannot return for them, and she becomes angry when his tone of voice hints that he does not think she is all that concerned. "It's OK…I've learned that sometimes I have to lower my standards," Jerry says, referring to their relationship. Jerry flies to Washington, D.C. to try to obtain government help to rescue the dogs. He is told that the soonest they can send out a plane is August. Jerry is distraught. "The dogs won't make it till August. I need a plane now!"

The scientist, who owes his very life to the heroism of the eight sled dogs, tells Jerry there is nothing he can do to help organize an expedition.

Jerry takes a job in the Pacific Northwest teaching children to kayak, and journeys to the man who sold him the dog team to ask his forgiveness. The dog trainer tells him to do whatever gives his heart rest. Jerry flies to New Zealand, knowing that somehow he has to get back to Antarctica as soon as possible.

Meanwhile, the eight dogs have waited for the humans to return to unchain them, and after several days, they realize they are on their own. All but one break

Paul Walker and friends in *Eight Below*

free or wriggle out of their collars. One stays behind to starve. The surviving seven must learn cooperative hunting techniques when they find that gulls are going to be their main source of food. The base's door blows off during a storm, and they find some crackers there to fend off starvation for a time. One dog dies after a fall from a cliff. While fighting off a vicious leopard seal to feed on an orca carcass, Maya is bitten and made half-lame. Young Max, the Malamute that Jerry had earlier called "all brawn and no brain," makes the most effort to help her and other fallen dogs. Now only six survive, and it is Max who, hearing the rumble of a motor approaching the base, wakes the others, who are now really feeling the toll of months of near starvation and hostile weather. Jerry's team has unexpectedly come to his rescue; Dr. McClaren has decided that the $200,000 remaining in his grant fund account should be spent on the dogs and Jerry. He pays Katie to fly out from New Zealand and land on an icebreaker, which carries them part of the way; the rest of journey is accomplished via an Italian snow cruiser.

Many elements of the original *Nankyoku Monogatari* were retained in this film, as when Jerry goes to the remote cabin of the man who bred the dogs used in his dog team, and expresses his shame at the way the dogs were abandoned. The humans stand by the scientific research station upon their return, pondering broken chains and the whereabouts of the dogs. They hear the distant bark of the dogs, which they interpret at first as their imagination. Then the dogs make their appearance dashing over a knoll. *Eight Below* continues the tradition of *Kelly and Me*, in which man and dog rescue one another; in the process the man (and, in *Eight Below*, the woman as well) grows and matures.

Rex takes a rest on Engine 55 in *Firehouse Dog*.

Firehouse Dog, a comedy about a canine movie star, whose credits include Jurassic Bark, that gets lost and finds himself working at a seedy fire station, was released in July 2007. In the story, Rexxx, an Irish Terrier (played by four terriers with *Lord of the Rings* names—Arwen, Frodo, Rohan and Stryder), is the most popular canine star in Hollywood. One day, an airplane stunt shot goes horribly wrong and he falls a thousand feet and disappears from the sight of the camera crew, losing his doggie toupe in the process. Presumed dead, Rexxx wanders to a suburban home in Dogpatch and is adopted by a young teenager whose father (Bruce Greenwood) takes him to his fire station number 55, which is to be closed due to its poor state of repair. Rexxx (now called Dewey) does some heroics in the line of duty and saves the station. His owner comes to the little town to claim him, and at first the dog voluntarily gets into his car.

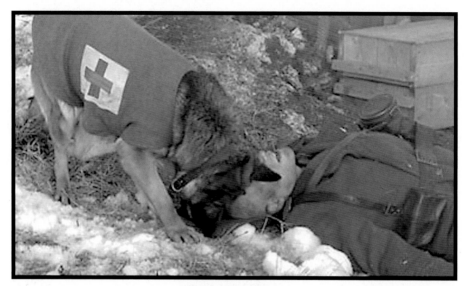

Finding Rin Tin Tin

However, that evening at their hotel, Rexxx hears the howl of the fire siren as his beloved new friends speed to the scene of a fire. He leaps from a balcony to join them. Rexxx has chosen the life of a real hero. Unfortunately, the film's script went for today's idea of comedy overflowing with potty humor—Rexxx poops in the firehouse chili. We'd rather watch Lassie reruns.

Finding Rin Tin Tin (2007), the true story of Rin-Tin-Tin, was filmed by the Bulgarian company Emmet/Furla Films in conjunction with Nu Image. Tyler Jensen, whose main claim to fame appears to be one episode of *Quintuplets*, portrays young airman Lee Duncan and acting vet Ben Cross appears as Nikolaus. The film was released theatrically in Germany, France and Canada and is available on DVD in the Netherlands and Germany. It is also available via download on the internet.

The legacy of those canine champions of the silver screen appears to be ageless. The Timeless Toy Company has even revived Rin-Tin-Tin as a stuffed toy, and Lassie Natural Way dog food, a new brand of pet food just appearing on supermarket shelves, is manufactured by Sunshine Mills, Inc., of Red Bay, Alabama.

If you suddenly got the urge to become a stage mother and make your precious pup into a hero of the silver screen, how would you go about it?

First, your dog would have to be trained in the basics. Fido will have to follow simple commands like "sit," "stay," "come," "down" and "no." After mastering these basic things, proceed to the intermediate level of tasks, such as fetch, jump over hurdles, walk correctly on a leash, ride in a car without whining or fidgeting, speak on command, find her "mark" as any actor would do, and wave.

The most advanced level comes next. Among these tasks are being able to follow the command "sic 'em," swim and do water stunts including rescue a victim, crawl, limp with one foot being favored (and always remember to favor the same foot) and knock a prop gun out of an actor's hand. Some dogs specialize in doing one or two difficult stunts like ladder climbing or water rescues so that they can be doubles or stunt dogs or do specialty commercials.

It must be pointed out that a movie dog won't be much of a movie star if she never does these tasks anywhere but her own backyard. Thus, a future doggie diva needs to become comfortable performing in front of a variety of people in a park, someone else's home, the beach or an auditorium.

The demand for trained dogs for commercials, comedies and dramas has never ceased. Dogs can be registered with various talent agencies, whether one's dog lives in California or New Hampshire. One of these agencies is Hollywood Animals of Los Angeles. Debra Marshall is a high school English teacher in southern California who has registered her Petit Basset Griffon Vendeen with

Hollywood Animals. Opus, says his owner, has a Benji look with lots of personality and an easygoing attitude. He is also a quick enough study.

"Personality is a must, I think," says Marshall:

> If they're not happy or energetic, the camera can tell. They must have basic behaviors, too, like sit and stay and be able to go to a mark. Fetching and waving, et cetera, are good, and any other cute tricks they can do, especially with hand signals. Opus knows lots of them, like being shot dead, playing the piano, putting a ball in a basket, and so on, and he'll do them for anyone…Opus also handles distractions well. If there's a treat to be had, he doesn't care how many people or what kind of equipment there might be around him—he just wants the food! And the better the treat, the more animated the performance.[3]

What is the true future of the dog hero in film and television?

The hero dog genre seems destined for comebacks, always ready to adapt to new forms of media. While the old dog hero of the 1920s and the 1970s, who had star billing in every one of his pictures, who posed with bathing beauties and movie moguls, and who endorsed dog flea soap, may be a relic of the past, no matter how jaded and cynical society becomes, few people can resist the charm of a cuddly, happy puppy. All film genres have their cycles, be it horror, Westerns, spy films, romantic comedies or super-hero action films. A genre becomes extremely popular when a film of that variety captures the audience's fancy. The popularity is often the result of memorable performances, a solid script, and social or cultural themes currently resonating with the message the film conveys. But then again, sometimes there is no explanation for the success of a motion picture or television show. Immediately Hollywood will begin throwing cheaply made imitations at the public until audiences grow so tired of them that the good films will be overlooked when fans stop spending their hard earned dollars on the genre. Once the imitator cycle begins, many films with a

similar theme will be produced and enthusiastically consumed as interest remains high until a critical point is reached when the film producers overfeed consumers with a genre or theme. But when this occurs cannot be predicted. Woe to the financial backers and the creative talent of a film released a few months after that critical moment when the cycle dies! But lack of interest will not last. All current and potential motion picture producers of dog hero films and television series, take heart! Time is on your side. Wait approximately 10 to 12 years, and a new generation will come into the world and your old product with new packaging will seem dramatically fresh.

It's almost certain that we won't get tired of seeing the cinematic dog hero yip, snarl, dig and swim for many decades to come, saving lives and property and delighting young and old.

A LIST OF FILMS
WITH DOG HEROES
AS MAJOR PROTAGONISTS,
AND THE DOGS PORTRAYING
THE HEROES

Ace

The Perils of Nyoka (available)

Almost a Gentleman

The Phantom (available)

The Monster Maker (available)

Jack London

The Rookie Cop (available)

Unsung Heroes

Apache

Eight Below (available)

Arwen

Firehouse Dog (available)

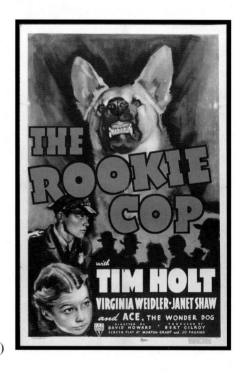

Asta

The Thin Man Goes Home (available)

Song of the Thin Man (available)

Shadow of the Thin Man (available)

Augustus von Schumacher

Won Ton Ton, the Dog Who Saved Hollywood

Baby

Lassie (television series, 1960—circa 1968) (available)

Baree
Baree, Son of Kazan

Bearheart
Legend of the Northwest (available)

Beasley
Turner and Hooch (available)

Beethoven
Beethoven (available)
Beethoven's 2nd (available)
Beethoven's 3rd (available)
Beethoven's 4th (available)

Benji
Benji: Off the Leash! (available)

Bingo
Bingo (available)

Blair
Rescued by Rover (available)

Caesar
Trailing the Killer (available)

Captain
Fighting to Live

Champion
Sky Rider (available)
Silent Sentinel

Conan
Eight Below (available)

The Dog Hero in Film

Dick
The Nobleman's Dog (available)

D. J.
Eight Below (available)

Dynamite
Wolf's Trail
Four-Footed Ranger
Hound of Silver Creek
Call of the Heart

Fang
The Range Riders
Sheriff's Girl

Fearless
The Silent Trailer (available)

Flame/Pal
Son of Rusty (available)
Rusty's Birthday (available)
Rusty Saves a Life
Out of the Blue
My Dog Shep
Dog of the Wild
Pal's Gallant Journey
I Found a Dog

Flash
Honeymoon
Shadows of the Night
Under the Black Eagle
Call the Mesquiteers (available)
The Flaming Signal (available)

Belgian poster for *Out of the Blue*

Floyd
Eight Below (available)

Friday
Eyes in the Night (available)
The Hidden Eye (available)

Frodo
Firehouse Dog (available)

Firehouse Dog

Gessa
The Call of the Wild: Dog of the Yukon (available)

Grief
Sein Bester Freund

Gustave
The Call of the Wild: Dog of the Yukon (available)

Higgins
Mooch Goes to Hollywood (available)
Benji (available)
Benji the Hunted (available)
For the Love of Benji (available)
Benji's Very Own Christmas Story (available)
Benji Takes a Dive at Marineland (available)

Jasper
Eight Below (available)

Jasper
Oh Heavenly Dog! (available)

Jean
Jean Goes Fishing
Where the Wind Blows
A Tin Type Romance
Jean Goes Foraging
Jean Rescues
Playmates
Jean, the Matchmaker
Jean Intervenes
Auld Lang Syne
The Signal of Distress
Jean and the Calico Doll
Jean and the Waif

Jed
White Fang (available)
The Journey of Natty Gann (available)

Jerry Lee
K 9 (available)
K 911 (available)
K 9: P. I. (available)

Kazan
Jaws of Justice (available)
Ferocious Pal
Outlaw's Highway

Kelly
Kelly and Me

Kelly

Kelly the Hero (television series, 1991) (available)

Klondike
The Law's Lash (available)
Marlie the Killer
Avenging Shadow
Fangs of Fate

Koda Bear
Eight Below (available)

Lad
Lad: A Dog

Lady
Fighting to Live

Lassie
Lassie (available)

Leader
The Return of Gray Wolf (available)

Lightnin'
Claws
Vengeance
Honor
Speed
Blitz
Lightnin' Wins
Lightnin' Strikes

Lightning
When Lightning Strikes (available)
Man's Best Friend
A Dog of Flanders (available)

Lightning Girl
Call of the Klondike (available)

London
The Littlest Hobo
The Littlest Hobo (television series, 1963—1964) (available)
My Dog Buddy

Mason
Lassie (available)

Mike
Sergeant Mike

Moose
The Wolf Man (available)
Frankenstein Meets the Wolf Man (available)

Muro
Untamed Justice
Sign of the Wolf (available)
Phantoms of the North

Nanette
Clash of the Wolves (available)
Where the North Begins (available)
Tracked By the Police (available)

Napoleon Bonaparte
The Thirteenth Hour (exists in a private archive)
Silent Hero
Danger Trail
Peacock Alley

Nikki
Nikki: Wild Dog of the North (available)

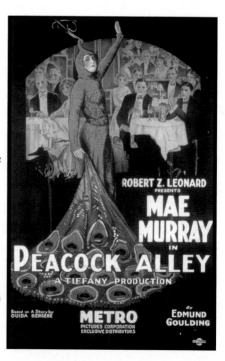

Noble
Eight Below (available)

Pal
Lassie Come Home (available)
Son of Lassie (available)
The Courage of Lassie (available)
Hills of Home (available)
Challenge to Lassie (available)
The Painted Hills (available)
The Sun Comes Up (available)
Lassie (television series, 1955 premiere) (available)

Pal, Jr.
Lassie (television series, 1955 — 1959) (available)

Peter The Great
The Silent Accuser
Wild Justice
Teasing Papa
Little Red Ridinghood
Sign of the Claw (available)
King of the Pack

Ranger
The One-Man Dog
Outlaw Dog
When a Dog Loves
Tracked (available)
Ranger of the North
Swift Shadow
Breed of Courage
Fangs of the Wild
The Law of Fear
Dog Law
Dog Justice

Rin-Tin-Tin (original)

Hello, Frisco

Where the North Begins (available)

Land of the Silver Fox

The Lighthouse by the Sea (available)

My Dad

Man From Hell's River

Shadows of the North

Rinty of the Desert

The Million Dollar Collar

A Dog of the Regiment

Clash of the Wolves (available)

The Night Cry (available)

A Hero of the Big Snows

Hills of Kentucky (available)

Tracked in the Snow Country

While London Sleeps

Below the Line

Jaws of Steel

A Race for Life

Find Your Man

The Show of Shows (available)

Frozen River

Tiger Rose (exists in the University of Wisconsin archives)

The Man Hunter

Rough Waters

On the Border

Tracked By the Police (available)

The Lone Defender, 1922

The Lone Defender, 1930 (available)

The Lightning Warrior (available)

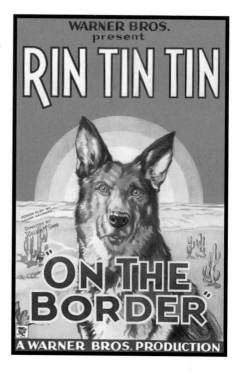

Rin-Tin-Tin IV

The Adventures of Rin-Tin-Tin (television series, 1954 premiere) (available)

Million Dollar Mermaid (available)

Rin-Tin-Tin, Jr.
The Adventures of Rex and Rinty
    (available)
The Test (available)
Pride of the Legion (available)
Skull and Crown (available)
Wolf Dog (available)
Law of the Wild (available)
Vengeance of Rannah (available)

Rocco
The Police Dog Story

Rohan
Firehouse Dog (available)

Sandow
The Call of the Wilderness
    (available)
Avenging Fangs

Saccha
White Fang to the Rescue (available)

Sgt. Rin-Tin-Tin III
The Return of Rin-Tin-Tin (available)

Shep
Dog of the Wild

Silverstreak
Fangs of Justice
The Silent Flyer (trailer available; film lost)

Silver Wolf
Radio Patrol (available)
Children of the Wild (available)

Sitka
Eight Below(available)

Skippy
The Thin Man (available)
After the Thin Man (available)
Another Thin Man (available)
Bringing Up Baby (available)

Spike
Old Yeller (available)

Spook
Lassie (television series, 1959—1960) (available)

Strongheart
North Star
Brawn of the North
The Love Master (exists in Paris' Archives du Film du CNC)
White Fang
The Silent Call
The Return of Boston Blackie (available)
The Warning

Stryder
Firehouse Dog (available)

Terry
The Wizard of Oz (available)

Thunder
His Master's Voice
The Silent Pal
Black Lightning
Phantom of the Forest
(exists in the
Library of
Congress archives)
Wings of the Storm
Wolf Fangs

Vosko
The Call of the Wild: Dog of the Yukon (available)

Wolf
Zurück aus dem Welthall (available)

Wolfheart
Wolfheart's Revenge (available)
Courage of Wolfheart
Fangs of Wolfheart
The Big Stunt

Yukon King
Sergeant Preston of the Yukon (television series, 1955—1958) (available)

Zandra
Paradise Valley

Zimbo
The Man Who Laughs (available)

FILMOGRAPHY

RESCUED BY ROVER (1905; CREDITS: Producer: Hepworth; Director: Cecil M. Hepworth and Lewin Fitzhamon; Screenplay: not known)

THE NOBLEMAN'S DOG (1909; CREDITS: Producer: Pathe; Director: uncredited; Screenplay: not known)

JEAN AND THE CALICO DOLL (1910; CREDITS: Producer: Vitagraph; Director: Lawrence Trimble; Screenplay: not known)

JEAN THE MATCHMAKER (1910; CREDITS: Producer: Vitagraph; Director: Lawrence Trimble; Screenplay: not known)

WHERE THE WIND BLOWS (1910; CREDITS: Producer: Vitagraph; Director: Lawrence Trimble; Screenplay: not known)

A TIN TYPE ROMANCE (1910; CREDITS: Producer: Vitagraph; Director: Lawrence Trimble; Screenplay: not known)

JEAN GOES FORAGING (1910; CREDITS: Producer: Vitagraph; Director: Lawrence Trimble; Screenplay: not known)

JEAN RESCUES (1911; CREDITS: Producer: Vitagraph; Director: Lawrence Trimble; Screenplay: not known)

AULD LANG SYNE (1911; CREDITS: Producer: Vitagraph; Director: Lawrence Trimble; Screenplay: not known)

JEAN GOES FISHING (1911; CREDITS: Producer: Vitagraph; Director: Lawrence Trimble; Screenplay: not known)

JEAN AND THE WAIF (1911; CREDITS: Producer: Vitagraph; Director: Lawrence Trimble; Screenplay: not known)

PLAYMATES (1911; CREDITS: Producer: Vitagraph; Director: Lawrence Trimble; Screenplay: not known)

JEAN INTERVENES (1912; CREDITS: Producer: Vitagraph; Director: Lawrence Trimble; Screenplay: not known)

THE SIGNAL OF DISTRESS (1912; CREDITS: Producer: Vitagraph; Director: Lawrence Trimble; Screenplay: not known)

BAREE, SON OF KAZAN (1918; CREDITS: Producer: Vitagraph; Director: David Smith; Screenplay: James Oliver Curwood)

THE SILENT CALL (1921; CREDITS: Producer: H. O. Davis; Director: Lawrence Trimble; Screenplay: Hal G. Evarts, Jane Murfin)

MY DAD (1922; CREDITS: Producer: Robertson-Cole Pictures Corporation; Director: Clifford Smith; Screenplay: Walter R. Hall, Richard Schayer)

MAN FROM HELL'S RIVER (1922; CREDITS: Producer: Irving Cummings Productions; Director: Irving Cummings; Screenplay: Irving Cummings, James Oliver Curwood)

BRAWN OF THE NORTH (1922; CREDITS: Producer: Trimble-Murfin Productions; Director: Lawrence Trimble; Screenplay: Philip Hubbard, Jane Murfin, Lawrence Trimble)

PEACOCK ALLEY (1922; CREDITS: Producer: Tiffany; Director: Robert Z. Leonard; Screenplay: Ouida Bergère, Edmund Goulding, Fanny Hatton)

THE LONE DEFENDER (1922; CREDITS: Producer: Film Booking Offices; Director: no director listed; Screenplay: not known)

WHERE THE NORTH BEGINS (1923; CREDITS: Producer: Warner Bros.; Director: Chester M. Franklin; Screenplay: Lee Duncan, Chester M. Franklin, Millard Webb, Raymond L. Schrock)

SHADOWS OF THE NORTH (1923; CREDITS: Producer: Universal; Director: Robert F. Hill; Screenplay: Edison Marshall, Paul Schofield)

TEASING PAPA (1923; CREDITS: Producer: Christie Comedies; Director: not known; Screenplay: not known)

BLACK LIGHTNING (1924; CREDITS: Producer: Gotham; Director: James P. Hogan; Screenplay: Harry Davis, Dorothy Howell)

FIND YOUR MAN (1924; CREDITS: Producer: Warner Bros.; Director: Malcolm St. Clair; Screenplay: Darryl F. Zanuck)

THE SILENT ACCUSER (1924; CREDITS: Producer: Metro Goldwyn Mayer; Directors: Chester M. Franklin and Frank O'Conner; Screenplay: Jack Boyle, Chester M. Franklin, Frank O'Conner)

THE LOVE MASTER (1924; CREDITS: Producer: Trimble-Murfin Productions/First National; Director: Lawrence Trimble; Screenplay: Donna Barrell, Joseph Barrell, Jane Murfin, Lawrence Trimble)

LITTLE RED RIDINGHOOD (1924; CREDITS: Producer: Century Film Company; Director: not known; Screenplay: not known)

HELLO, FRISCO (1924; CREDITS: Producer: Universal; Director: Slim Summerville; Screenplay: not known)

THE LIGHTHOUSE BY THE SEA (1924; CREDITS: Producer: Warner Bros.; Director: Malcolm St. Clair; Screenplay: Owen Davis and Darryl F. Zanuck)

WILD JUSTICE (1925; CREDITS: Producer: United Picture Artists; Director: Chester M. Franklin; Screenplay: C. Gardner Sullivan)

CLASH OF THE WOLVES (1925; CREDITS: Producer: Warner Bros.; Director: Noel M. Smith; Screenplay: Charles Logue)

NORTH STAR (1925; CREDITS: Producer: Howard Estabrook Productions; Director: Paul Powell; Screenplay: Charles Horan, Rufus King)

WHITE FANG (1925; CREDITS: Producer: Trimble-Murfin Productions/First National; Director: Lawrence Trimble; Screenplay; Jane Murfin)

TRACKED IN THE SNOW COUNTRY (1925; CREDITS: Producer: Warner Bros.; Director: Herman C. Raymaker; Screenplay: Herman C. Raymaker, Edward J. Meagher)

CLAWS (1925; CREDITS: Producer: Sun Pictures Corporation; Director: James Vincent; Screenplay: not known)

VENGEANCE (1925; CREDITS: Producer: Sun Pictures Corporation; Director: James Vincent; Screenplay: not known)

HONOR (1925; CREDITS: Producer: Sun Pictures Corporation; Director: James Vincent; Screenplay: not known)

THE BIG STUNT (1925; CREDITS: Producer: Charles R. Seeling Productions; Director: Charles R. Seeling; Screenplay: not known)

BELOW THE LINE (1925; CREDITS: Producer: Warner Bros.; Director: Herman C. Raymaker; Screenplay: Charles Logue)

HIS MASTER'S VOICE (1925; CREDITS: Producer: Gotham; Director: Renaud Hoffman; Screenplay: Frank Foster Davis, Henry McCarty, James J. Tynan)

THE SILENT PAL (1925; CREDITS: Producer: Gotham; Director: Henry McCarty; Screenplay: Henry McCarty)

WOLFHEART'S REVENGE (1925; CREDITS: Producer: Charles R. Seeling Productions; Director: Charles R. Seeling; Screenplay: not known)

COURAGE OF WOLFHEART (1925; CREDITS: Producer: Charles R. Seeling Productions; Director: Charles R. Seeling; Screenplay: not known)

FANGS OF WOLFHEART (1925; CREDITS: Producer: Charles R. Seeling Productions; Director: Charles R. Seeling; Screenplay: not known)

SHERIFF'S GIRL (1926; CREDITS: Producer: Ben Wilson Productions; Director: Ben F. Wilson; Screenplay: not known)

THE RETURN OF GRAY WOLF (1926; CREDITS: Producer: Ambassador Pictures; Director: Jack Rollens; Screenplay: not known)

CALL OF THE KLONDIKE (1926; CREDITS: Producer: Paul Gerson Pictures; Director: Oscar Apfel; Screenplay: Jack Natleford)

LIGHTNIN' STRIKES (1926; CREDITS: Producer: Tenneck Pictures; Director: no director credited; Screenplay: not known)

SIGN OF THE CLAW (1926; CREDITS: Producer: Gotham; Director: B. Reeves Eason; Screenplay: James Bell Smith)

KING OF THE PACK (1926; CREDITS: Producer: Gotham; Director: Frank Richardson; Screenplay: James Bell Smith, Delos Sutherland)

THE NIGHT CRY (1926; CREDITS: Producer: Warner Bros.; Director: Herman C. Raymaker; Screenplay: Ewart Adamson, Paul Klein, Edward Meagher)

A HERO OF THE BIG SNOWS (1926; CREDITS: Producer: Warner Bros.; Director: Herman C. Raymaker; Screenplay: Ewart Adamson)

THE CALL OF THE WILDERNESS (1926; CREDITS: Producer: Associated Exhibitors; Director: Jack Nelson; Screenplay: Earl Johnson, Lon Young)

THE SILENT TRAILER (1926; CREDITS: Producer: Van Pelt Brothers; Director: Joe Rock; Screenplay: not known)

THE MOUNTAIN EAGLE, (1926; CREDITS: Producer: Gainsborough Pictures; Director: Alfred Hitchcock; Screenplay: Max Ferner, Charles Lapworth, Eliot Stannard)

SPEED (1926; CREDITS: Producer: Sun Pictures Corporation; Director: James Vincent; Screenplay: not known)

BLITZ (1926; CREDITS: Producer: Sun Pictures Corporation; Director: James Vincent; Screenplay: not known)

WINGS OF THE STORM (1926; CREDITS: Producer: Fox; Director: John G. Blystone; Screenplay: Elizabeth Pickett, Gordon Rigby, Dorothy Yost)

WHILE LONDON SLEEPS (1926; CREDITS: Producer: Warner Bros.; Director: Howard Bretherton; Screenplay: Walter Morosco)

FANGS OF JUSTICE (1926; CREDITS: Producer: Samuel Bischoff Productions; Director: Noel M. Smith; Screenplay: Adele De Vore)

THE SILENT FLYER (1926; CREDITS: Producer: Mascot Pictures Corporation; Director: William James Craft; Screenplay: George Morgan)

THE RETURN OF BOSTON BLACKIE (1927; CREDITS: Producer: Chadwick Pictures Corporation; Director: Harry O. Hoyt; Screenplay: Leah Baird, Jack Boyle)

THE WARNING (1927; CREDITS: Producer: Columbia Pictures Corporation; Director: George B. Seitz; Screenplay: Lillian Ducey, H. Milber Kitchin, George B. Seitz)

THE RANGE RIDERS (1927; CREDITS: Producer: Ben Wilson Productions/Rayart Pictures; Director: Ben F. Wilson; Screenplay: Robert Dillon, Earl Turner)

WOLF FANGS (1927; CREDITS: Producer: Fox; Director: Lewis Seiler; Screenplay: Seton I. Miller, Elizabeth Pickett)

AVENGING FANGS (1927; CREDITS: Producer: Chesterfield Motion Picture Corporation; Director: Ernest van Pelt; Screenplay: George W. Pyper)

WOLF'S TRAIL (1927; CREDITS: Producer: Universal; Director: Francis Ford; Screenplay: Gardner Bradford, Basil Dickey)

THE THIRTEENTH HOUR (1927; CREDITS: Producer: Metro Goldwyn Mayer; Director: Chester M. Franklin; Screenplay: Chester M. Franklin, Douglas Furber, Edward T. Lowe, Jr., Wellyn Totman)

SILENT HERO (1927; CREDITS: Producer: Duke Worne Productions; Director: Duke Worne; Screenplay: George W. Pyper, H.H. van Coan)

OUTLAW DOG (1927; CREDITS: Producer: Robertson-Cole Pictures Corporation; Director: J. P. McGowan; Screenplay: Ewart Adamson, F.A.E. Pine)

WHEN A DOG LOVES (1927; CREDITS: Producer: Robertson-Cole Pictures Corporation; Director: J. P. McGowan; Screenplay: John A. Moroso, F.A.E. Pine)

THE SWIFT SHADOW (1927; CREDITS: Producer: Robertson-Cole Pictures Corporation; Director: Jerome Storm; Screenplay: Ethel Hill)

BREED OF COURAGE (1927; CREDITS: Producer: Robertson-Cole Pictures Corporation; Director: Howard M. Mitchell; Screenplay: Leon D'Usseau, F.A.E. Pine, John Twist)

JAWS OF STEEL (1927; CREDITS: Producer: Warner Bros.; Director: Ray Enright; Screenplay: Charles R. Condon, Darryl F. Zanuck)

TRACKED BY THE POLICE (1927; CREDITS: Producer: Warner Bros.; Director: Ray Enright; Screenplay: John Grey, Darryl F. Zanuck)

A DOG OF THE REGIMENT (1927; CREDITS: Producer: Warner Bros.; Director: D. Ross Lederman; Screenplay: Charles R. Condon, Albert S. Howson)

HILLS OF KENTUCKY (1927; CREDITS: Producer: Warner Bros.; Director: Howard Bretherton; Screenplay: Edward Clark, Dorothy Yost)

HONEYMOON (1928; CREDITS: Producer: Metro Goldwyn Mayer; Director: Robert A. Golden; Screenplay: Robert E. Hopkins, Lew Lipton, George O'Hara, Richard Schayer)

TRACKED (1928; CREDITS: Producer: Robertson-Cole Pictures Corporation; Director: Jerome Storm; Screenplay: Frank Howard Clark, Helen Gregg, John Twist)

RANGER OF THE NORTH (1928; CREDITS: Producer: Robertson-Cole Pictures Corporation; Director: Jerome Storm; Screenplay: Ewart Adamson, Leon D'Usseau)

FANGS OF THE WILD (1928; CREDITS: Producer: Robertson-Cole Pictures Corporation; Director: Jerome Storm; Screenplay: Randolph Bartlett, Dwight Cummins, Ethel Hill, Dorothy Yost)

LAW OF FEAR (1928; CREDITS: Producer: Robertson-Cole Pictures Corporation; Director: Jerome Storm; Screenplay: Randolph Bartlett, William Francis Dugan, Ethel Hill)

DOG LAW (1928; CREDITS: Producer: Film Booking Offices (FBO); Director: Jerome Storm; Screenplay: Frank Howard Clark, Helen Gregg, E. V. Taylor)

DOG JUSTICE (1928; CREDITS: Producer: Film Booking Offices (FBO); Director: Jerome Storm; Screenplay: Randolph Bartlett, Ethel Hill)

SKY RIDER (1928; CREDITS: Producer: Chesterfield Motion Picture Corporation; Director: Alan James; Screenplay: Alan James, Lon Young)

SILENT SENTINEL (1928; CREDITS: Producer: Chesterfield Motion Pictures Corporation; Director: Alan James; Screenplay: Alan James)

FOUR-FOOTED RANGER (1928; CREDITS: Producer: Universal; Director: Stuart Paton; Screenplay: Gardner Bradford, Paul M. Bryan, Cromwell Kent)

HOUND OF SILVER CREEK (1928; CREDITS: Producer: Universal; Director: Stuart Paton; Screenplay: Gardner Bradford, Paul M. Bryan)

SHADOWS OF THE NIGHT (1928; CREDITS: Producer: Metro Goldwyn Mayer; Director: D. Ross Lederman; Screenplay: Robert E. Hopkins, D. Ross Lederman, Ted Shane)

UNDER THE BLACK EAGLE (1928; CREDITS: Producer: Metro Goldwyn Mayer; Director: W. S. van Dyke; Screenplay: Norman Houston, Bradley King, Madeline Ruthven)

THE LAW'S LASH (1928; CREDITS: Producer: Fred J. McConnell Productions; Director: Noel M. Smith; Screenplay: Edward J. Meagher, George W. Pyper)

MARLIE THE KILLER (1928; CREDITS: Producer: Fred J. McConnell Productions; Director: Noel M. Smith; Screenplay: Hazel Christie McDonald, George W. Pyper)

AVENGING SHADOW (1928; CREDITS: Producer: Fred J. McConnell Productions; Director: Ray Taylor; Screenplay: Bennett Cohen)

FANGS OF FATE (1928; CREDITS: Producer: Fred J. McConnell; Director: Noel M. Smith; Screenplay: Arthur Q. Hagerman, Earl Johnson, Jack Kelly)

LAND OF THE SILVER FOX (1928; CREDITS: Producer: Warner Bros.; Director: Ray Enright; Screenplay: Charles R. Condon, Joseph Jackson, Howard Smith)

RINTY OF THE DESERT (1928; CREDITS: Producer: Warner Bros.; Director: D. Ross Lederman; Screenplay: Harvey Gates, James A. Starr, Frank Steele)

A RACE FOR LIFE (1928; CREDITS: Producer: Warner Bros.; Director: R. Ron Lederman; Screenplay: Charles R. Condon, James A. Starr)

THE MAN WHO LAUGHS (1928; CREDITS: Producer: Universal; Director: Paul Leni; Screenplay: J. Grubb Alexander, Walter Anthony, May McLean)

CALL OF THE HEART (1929; CREDITS: Producer: Universal; Director: Francis Ford)

THE ONE-MAN DOG (1929; CREDITS: Producer: Robertson-Cole Pictures Corporation; Director: Leon D'Usseau; Screenplay: Frank Howard Clark, Helen Gregg)

THE SHOW OF SHOWS (1929; CREDITS: Producer: Warner Bros.; Director: John G. Adolfi; Screenplay: J. Keirn Brannan, Frank Fay)

FROZEN RIVER (1929; CREDITS: Producer: Warner Bros.; Director: F. Harmon Weight; Screenplay: Harry Behn, Anthony Coldeway, John F. Fowler, James A. Starr)

TIGER ROSE (1929; CREDITS: Producer: Warner Bros.; Director: George Fitzmaurice; Screenplay: DeLeon Anthony, Willard Mack, Bordon Rigby, Harvey F. Thew)

THE MILLION DOLLAR COLLAR (1929; CREDITS: Producer: Warner Bros.; Director: D. Ross Lederman; Screenplay: Robert Lord, James A. Starr)

PHANTOMS OF THE NORTH (1929; CREDITS: Producer: All-Star Productions; Director: Harry S. Webb; Screenplay: F.E. Douglas, George C. Hull, Carl Krusada)

SEIN BESTER FREUND (1929; CREDITS: Producer: Ariel Film; Director: Harry Piel; Screenplay: Hans Raneau)

UNTAMED JUSTICE (1929; CREDITS: Producer: Biltmore Productions; Director: Harry S. Webb; Screenplay: Jack Natteford)

LIGHTNIN' WINS (1929; CREDITS: Producer: Sun Pictures Corporation; Director: James Vincent; Screenplay: not known)

DANGER TRAIL (1929; CREDITS: Producer: Richard Talmadge Productions; Director: Noel M. Smith; Screenplay: not known)

THE MAN HUNTER (1930; CREDITS: Producer: Warner Bros.; Director: D. Ross Lederman; Screenplay: Lillie Hayward, James A. Starr)

ROUGH WATERS (1930; CREDITS: Producer: Warner Bros.; Director: John Daumery; Screenplay: James A. Starr)

ON THE BORDER (1930; CREDITS: Producer: Warner Bros.; Director: William C. McGann; Screenplay: Lillie Hayward)

THE LONE DEFENDER (1931; CREDITS: Producer: Mascot; Director: Richard Thorpe; Screenplay: William P. Burt, Bennett Cohen, Harry L. Fraser)

SIGN OF THE WOLF (1931; CREDITS: Producer: Metropolitan Pictures Corporation; Directors: Harry F. Webb and Forrest Sheldon; Screenplay: Betty Burbidge, Bennett Cohen, Carl Krusada)

THE LIGHTNING WARRIOR (1931; CREDITS: Producer: Mascot; Director: Benjamin H. Kline and Armand Schaefer; Screenplay: Ford Beebe, Colbert Clark, Wyndham Gittens)

TRAILING THE KILLER (1932; CREDITS: Producer: Trem Carr Productions, Ltd.; Director: Herman C. Raymaker; Screenplay: Jackson Richards)

PRIDE OF THE LEGION (1932; CREDITS: Producer: Mascot; Director: Ford Beebe; Screenplay: Ford Beebe, Peter B. Kyne)

THE FLAMING SIGNAL (1932; CREDITS: Producer: Imperial Productions, Inc.; Director: George Jeske and Charles E. Roberts; Screenplay: Thomas Hughes, Charles E. Roberts, William G. Stever)

JAWS OF JUSTICE (1933; CREDITS: Producer: Principal Pictures Corporation; Director: Spencer Gordon Bennet; Screenplay: Joseph Anthony Roach)

WOLF DOG (1933; CREDITS: Producer: Mascot; Director: Colbert Clark and Harry L. Fraser; Screenplay: Colbert Clark, Wyndham Gittens, Sherman L. Lowe, Al Martin, Barney A. Sarecky)

THE THIN MAN (1934; CREDITS: Producer: MGM; Director: W. S. van Dyke; Screenplay: Dashiell Hammett, Albert Hackett, Frances Goodrich)

PARADISE VALLEY (1934; CREDITS: Producer: Imperial Productions; Director: James P. Hogan; Screenplay: Ira Anson, George Arthur Durham, Frances Wheeler)

FIGHTING TO LIVE (1934; CREDITS: Producer: Principal Pictures Corporation; Director: Edward F. Cline; Screenplay: Robert Ives)

FEROCIOUS PAL (1934; CREDITS: Producer: Principal Pictures Corporation; Director: Spencer Gordon Bennet; Screenplay: Joseph Anthony Roach)

INSIDE INFORMATION (1934; CREDITS: Producer: Stage and Screen Productions; Director: Robert F. Hill; Screenplay: Bert Ennis and Victor Potel)

OUTLAW'S HIGHWAY (1934; CREDITS: Producer: Trop Productions; Director: Robert F. Hill; Screenplay: Myron Dattlebaum)

WHEN LIGHTNING STRIKES (1934; CREDITS: Producer: Regal Productions; Director: Harry Revier; Screenplay: George Morgan)

THE TEST (1935; CREDITS: Producer: Mascot; Directors: Ford Beebe and B. Reeves Eason; Screenplay: James Oliver Curwood)

SKULL AND CROWN (1935; CREDITS: Producer: Reliable; Director: Elmer Clifton; Screenplay: Bennett Cohen, James Oliver Curwood, Carl Krusada)

MAN'S BEST FRIEND (1935; CREDITS: Producer: Johnson-Kull Productions; Directors: Edward A. Kull and Thomas Storey; Screenplay: Thomas Storey)

A DOG OF FLANDERS (1935; CREDITS: Producer: RKO; Director: Edward Sloman; Screenplay: Dorothy Yost)

THE ADVENTURES OF REX AND RINTY (1935; CREDITS: Producer: Mascot; Director: Ford Beebe; Screenplay: B. Reeves Eason, Maurice Geraghty, John Rothwell, Barney Sarecky)

CHILDREN OF THE WILD (1935; CREDITS: Producer: Pennant Pictures Corporation; Director: Charles Hutchinson; Screenplay: not known)

LAW OF THE WILD (1936; CREDITS: Producer: Mascot; Directors: B. Reeves Eason and Armand Schaefer; Screenplay: Ford Beebe, B. Reeves Eason, Sherman L. Lowe, Al Martin, John Rothwell)

THE VENGEANCE OF RANNAH (1936; CREDITS: Producer: Reliable; Director: Bernard B. Ray; Screenplay: James Oliver Curwood, Joseph O'Donnell

THE VOICE OF BUGLE ANN (1936; CREDITS: Producer: MGM; Director: Richard Thorpe; Screenplay: Harvey Gates, Samuel Hoffenstein)

RADIO PATROL (1937; CREDITS: Producer: Universal; Directors: Ford Beebe and Clifford Smith; Screenplay: Wyndham Gittens, Norman S. Hall, Charlie Schmidt, Eddie Sullivan, Ray Trappe)

AFTER THE THIN MAN (1938; CREDITS: Producer: MGM; Director: W. S. van Dyke; Screenplay: Frances Goodrich, Albert Hackett)

BLIND ALIBI (1938; CREDITS: Producer: RKO; Director: Lew Landers; Screenplay: William J. Cowan, Lionel Howser)

BRINGING UP BABY (1938; CREDITS: Producer: RKO; Director: Howard Hawks; Screenplay: Hagar Wilde, Dudley Nichols)

CALL THE MESQUITEERS (1938; CREDITS: Producer: Republic; Director: John English; Screenplay: William Colt McDonald, Bernard McConville, Luci Ward)

ALMOST A GENTLEMAN (1939; CREDITS: Producer: RKO; Director: Leslie Goodwins; Screenplay: Harold Shumate, David Silverstein, Jo Pagano)

THE ROOKIE COP (1939; CREDITS: Producer: RKO; Director: David Howard; Screenplay: Guy K. Austin, Morton Grant, Earl Johnson, Jo Pagano)

THE WIZARD OF OZ (1939); CREDITS: Producer: Metro Goldwyn Mayer; Director: Victor Fleming; Screenplay: Noel Langley, Florence Ryerson, Edgar Allan Woolf)

ANOTHER THIN MAN (1939; CREDITS: Producer: Metro Goldwyn Mayer; Director: W. S. van Dyke; Screenplay: Dashiell Hammett, Frances Goodrich, Albert Hackett).

SILVER STALLION (1941; CREDITS: Producer: Boots and Saddles Productions; Director: Edward Finney; Screenplay: Robert Emmett Tansey)

THE WOLF MAN (1941; CREDITS: Producer: Universal Pictures; Director: George Waggner; Screenplay: Curt Siodmak)

SHADOW OF THE THIN MAN (1941; CREDITS: Producer: Metro Goldwyn Mayer; Director: W. S. van Dyke; Screenplay: Harry Kurnitz, Irving Brecher)

EYES IN THE NIGHT (1942; CREDITS: Producer: Metro Goldwyn Mayer; Director: Fred Zinnemann; Screenplay: Baynard Kendrick, Guy Trosper, Howard Emmett Rogers)

THE PERILS OF NYOKA (1942; CREDITS: Producer: Republic; Director: William Witney; Screenplay: Ronald Davidson, Norman S. Hall, William Lindy, Joseph O'Donnell, Joseph F. Odal)

UNSUNG HEROES (1942; CREDITS: Producer: Monogram; Director: S. Roy Lusby; Screenplay: Ande Lamb, John Vlahos)

FRANKENSTEIN MEETS THE WOLF MAN (1943; CREDITS: Producer: Universal; Director: Ray William Neill; Screenplay: Curt Siodmak)

LASSIE COME HOME (1943; CREDITS: Producer: Metro Goldwyn Mayer; Director: Fred M. Wilcox; Screenplay: Hugo Butler)

JACK LONDON (1943; CREDITS: Producer: Samuel Bronston Productions; Director: Alfred Santell; Screenplay: Isaac Don Levine, Ernest Pascal)

THE MONSTER MAKER (1944; CREDITS: Producer: Producers Releasing Corporation; Director: Sam Newfield; Screenplay: Pierre Gendron, Martin Mooney, Lawrence Williams)

THE PHANTOM (1944; CREDITS: Producer: Columbia Pictures Corporation; Director: B. Reeves Eason; Screenplay: Morgan Cox, Sherman L. Lowe, Victor McLeod, Leslie Swabacker)

SERGEANT MIKE (1944; CREDITS: Producer: Columbia Pictures Corporation; Director: Henry Levin; Screenplay: Robert Lee Johnson)

THE THIN MAN GOES HOME (1944; CREDITS: Producer: MGM; Director: Richard Thorpe; Screenplay: Robert Riskin, Harry Kurnitz, Dwight Taylor)

THE HIDDEN EYE (1945; CREDITS: Producer: Metro Goldwyn Mayer; Director: Richard Whorf; Screenplay: George Harmon Coxe, Baynard Kendrick, Harry Ruskin)

THE ADVENTURES OF RUSTY (1945; CREDITS: Producer: Darmour Inc/Columbia Pictures; Director: Paul Burnford; Screenplay: Al Martin and Aubrey Wisberg)

SON OF LASSIE (1945; CREDITS: Producer: Metro Goldwyn Mayer; Director: S. Sylvan Simon; Jeanne Bartlett, Eric Knight)

THE COURAGE OF LASSIE (1946; CREDITS: Producer: Metro Goldwyn Mayer; Director: Fred M. Wilcox; Screenplay: Lionel Houser)

GOD'S COUNTRY (1946; CREDITS: Producer: Screen Guild Productions; Director: Robert Emmett Tansey; Screenplay: James Oliver Curwood, Frances Kavenaugh)

IT SHOULDN'T HAPPEN TO A DOG (1946; CREDITS: Producer; 20th Century Fox; Director: Herbert J. Leeds; Screenplay: Frank Gabrielsen, Edwin Lanham)

THE RETURN OF RIN-TIN-TIN (1947; CREDITS: Producer: Romay Pictures; Director: Max Nosseck; Screenplay: Jack DeWitt, William Stephens)

SONG OF THE THIN MAN (1947; CREDITS: Producer: Metro Goldwyn Mayer; Director: Edward Buzzell; Screenplay: Dashiell Hammett, Stanley Roberts, Steve Fisher, Nat Perrin)

OUT OF THE BLUE (1947; CREDITS: Producer: Eagle-Lion Films; Director: Leigh Jason; Screenplay: Walter Bullock, Vera Caspary, Edward Eliscot)

MY DOG SHEP (1947; CREDITS: Producer: Golden Gate Pictures; Director: Ford Beebe; Screenplay: Ford Beebe)

SON OF RUSTY (1947; CREDITS: Producer: Columbia Pictures Corporation; Director: Lew Landers; Screenplay: Malcolm Stewart Boylan, Al Martin)

THE TENDER YEARS (1948; CREDITS: Producer: 20th Century Fox; Director: Harold B. Schuster; Screenplay: Arnold Belgasrd, Abern Finkel)

RUSTY'S BIRTHDAY (1949; CREDITS: Producer: Columbia, Pictures Corporation; Director: Seymour Friedman; Screenplay: Al Martin, Brenda Weisberg)

RUSTY SAVES A LIFE (1949; CREDITS: Producer: Columbia Pictures Corporation; Director: Seymour Friedman; Screenplay: Al Martin, Brenda Weisberg)

DOG OF THE WILD (1949; CREDITS: Producer: RKO; Director: Richard Irving; Screenplay: Hattie Bilson)

PAL'S GALLANT JOURNEY (1949; CREDITS: Producer: RKO; Director: Richard Irving; Screenplay: George Bilson)

I FOUND A DOG (1949; CREDITS: Producer: RKO; Director: Lew Landers; Screenplay: Hattie Bilson)

CHALLENGE TO LASSIE (1949; CREDITS: Producer: Metro Goldwyn Mayer; Director: Richard Thorpe; Screenplay: Eleanor Atkinson, William Ludwig)

HILLS OF HOME (1949; CREDITS: Producer: Metro Goldwyn Mayer; Director: Fred M. Wilcox; Screenplay: William Ludwig, Ian Maclaren)

THE SUN COMES UP (1949; CREDITS: Producer: Metro Goldwyn Mayer; Director: Richard Thorpe; Screenplay: Margaret Fitts, William Ludwig)

THE PAINTED HILLS (1951; CREDITS: Producer: Metro Goldwyn Mayer; Director: Harold M. Kress; Screenplay: Alexander Hull, True Boardman)

MILLION DOLLAR MERMAID (1952; CREDITS: Producer: Metro Goldwyn Mayer; Director: Mervyn LeRoy; Screenplay: Everett Freeman)

THE ADVENTURES OF RIN-TIN-TIN (1954-1959; CREDITS: Producer: Screen Gems Television; Directors: Earl Bellamy and Charles S. Gould; Screenplays: Lee Borg, Jennings Cobb, Ray Erwin, Douglas Hayes, Hugh King)

LASSIE (1954-1974; CREDITS: Producer: Robert Maxwell Associates and Wrather Productions; Directors: William Beaudine and William Beaudine, Jr.; Screenplays: John McGreevey, Eric Scott, Mercy Weireter)

SERGEANT PRESTON OF THE YUKON (1955-1958; CREDITS: Producer: Trendle-Campbell-Meurer, Incorporated; Directors: Earl Bellamy and Eddie Dean; Screenplays: Dwight V. Babcock, Eric Freiwald)

EDGE OF HELL (1956; CREDITS: Producer: Universal; Director: Hugo Haas; Screenplay: Hugo Haas)

OLD YELLER (1957; CREDITS: Producer: Walt Disney Pictures; Director: Robert Stevenson; Screenplay: Fred Gipson and William Tunberg)

KELLY AND ME (1957; CREDITS: Producer: Universal-International; Director: Robert Z. Leonard; Screenplay: Everett Freeman)

THE LITTLEST HOBO (1958; CREDITS: Producer: Allied Artists; Director: Charles R, Rondeau; Screenplay: Dorrell McGowan)

ZURÜCK AUS DEM WELTALL (MOON WOLF) (1959; CREDITS: Producer: Alfa Film; Director: Georges Friedland; Screenplay: Georges Friedland, Johannes Kendrick)

MY DOG BUDDY (1960; CREDITS: Producer: Columbia Pictures/McLendon Radio Pictures; Director: Ray Kellogg; Screenplay: Ray Kellogg)

NIKKI: WILD DOG OF THE NORTH (1961; CREDITS: Producer: Walt Disney Pictures; Directors: Jack Couffer and Don Haldane; Screenplay: James Oliver Curwood, Dwight Hauser)

THE POLICE DOG STORY (1961; CREDITS: Producer: Zenith; Director: Edward L. Cahn; Screenplay: Orville H. Hampton)

THE SILENT CALL (1961; CREDITS: Producer: 20th Century Fox/Associated Producers, Incorporated; Director: John A. Bushelman; Screenplay: Hal G. Evarts, Tom Maruzzi)

LAD, A DOG (1962; CREDITS: Producer: Warner Bros./Vanguard Productions; Directors: Aram Avakian and Leslie H. Martinson; Screenplay: Lillie Hayward, Albert Payson Terhune)

THE LITTLEST HOBO (1963; CREDITS: Producer: Storer Programs, Incorporated; Director: Dick Darley and Phyllis Hirsch; Screenplays: Barbara Merlin and Milton Merlin)

MOOCH GOES TO HOLLYWOOD (1971; CREDITS: Producer: Greenlight Pictures; Director: Richard Erdman; Screenplay: Jim Backus, Jerry Devine)

ZANNA BIANCA (1973; CREDITS: Producer: Cine Compania Industrial Cinematografica; Director: Lucio Fulci; Screenplay: Guy Elmas, Roberto Gianviti, Thom Keyes, Piero Regnoli, Guillaume Roux, Harry Alan Townes)

ZANNA BIANCA ALLA RISCOSSA (1974; CREDITS: Producer: Cine Compania Industrial Cinematografica; Director: Tonino Ricci; Screenplay: Sandro Continenza, Giovanni Simonelli)

BENJI (1974; CREDITS: Producer: Mulberry Square Productions; Director: Joe Camp; Screenplay: Joe Camp)

WON TON TON, THE DOG WHO SAVED HOLLYWOOD (1976; CREDITS: Producer: Paramount Pictures; Director: Michael Winner; Screenplay: Arnold Schulman, Cy Howard)

BENJI THE HUNTED (1977; CREDITS: Producer: Mulberry Square Productions/Walt Disney Pictures; Director: Joe Camp; Screenplay: Joe Camp)

FOR THE LOVE OF BENJI (1977; CREDITS: Producer: Mulberry Square Productions; Director: Joe Camp; Screenplay: Joe Camp)

BENJI'S VERY OWN CHRISTMAS STORY (1978; CREDITS: Producer: Mulberry Square Productions; Director: Joe Camp; Screenplay: Joe Camp, Dan Witt)

LEGEND OF THE NORTHWEST (1978; CREDITS: Producer: Rand Productions, Incorporated; Director: Rand Brooks; Screenplay: Rand Brooks, Jennings Cobb)

OH HEAVENLY DOG! (1980; CREDITS: Producer: 20th Century Fox/Mulberry Square Productions; Director: Joe Camp; Screenplay: Rod Browning)

BENJI TAKES A DIVE AT MARINELAND (1981; CREDITS: Producer: American Broadcasting Corporation; Director: none listed; Screenplay: none listed)

THE JOURNEY OF NATTY GANN (1985; CREDITS: Producer: Walt Disney Pictures; Director: Jeremy Paul Kagan; Screenplay: Jeanne Rosenberg)

TURNER AND HOOCH (1989; CREDITS: Producer: Touchstone Pictures; Director: Roger Spottsiwoode; Screenplay: Dennis Shryack. Michael Blodgett, Daniel Petrie, Jr., Jim Cash, Jack Epps, Jr.)

K-9 (1989; CREDITS: Producer: Universal; Director: Rod Daniel; Screenplay: Steven Siegel, Scott Myers)

BINGO (1991; CREDITS: Producer: TriStar Pictures; Director: Matthew Robbins; Screenplay: Jim Strain)

KELLY THE HERO (1991; CREDITS: Producer: Westbridge Entertainment/Film Victoria; Directors: Brendan Maher, Mike Smith, Paul Moloney, Mark Defriest and Chris Langman; Screenplays: not listed)

WHITE FANG (1991; CREDITS: Producer: Hybrid Productions/Walt Disney Pictures; Director: Randal Kleiser; Screenplay: Jeanne Rosenberg, Nick Thiel, David Fallon)

BEETHOVEN (1992; CREDITS: Producer: Northern Lights Entertainment/Universal Pictures; Director: Brian Levant; Screenplay: John Hughes, Amy Holden Jones)

BEETHOVEN'S 2ND (1993; CREDITS: Producer: Universal; Director: Rod Daniel; Screenplay: John Hughes, Amy Holden Jones, Len Blum)

WHITE FANG II: MYTH OF THE WHITE WOLF (1994; CREDITS: Producer: Walt Disney Pictures/Hiro Narita, Preston Fischer, Justin Greene and David Fallon; Director: Ken Olin; Screenplay: David Fallon)

LASSIE (1994; CREDITS: Producer: Broadway Pictures/Paramount Pictures; Director: Daniel Petrie; Screenplay: Matthew Jacobs, Gary Ross, Elizabeth Anderson)

THE CALL OF THE WILD: DOG OF THE YUKON (1997; CREDITS: Producer: Kingsborough; Director: Peter Svatek; Screenplay: Graham Ludlow)

K-911 (1999; CREDITS: Producer: Universal; Director: Charles T. Kanganis; Screenplay: Steven Siegel, Scott Myers, Cary Scott Thompson)

BEETHOVEN'S 3RD (2000; CREDITS: Producer: Universal; Director: David M. Evans; Screenplay: John Hughes, Amy Holden Jones, Jeff Schechter)

BEETHOVEN'S 4TH (2001; CREDITS: Producer: Universal; Director: David M. Evans; Screenplay: John Hughes, Amy Holden Jones, John Loy)

K-9: P.I. (2002; CREDITS: Producer: Universal; Director: Richard S. Lewis; Screenplay: Steven Siegel, Scott Myers, Gary Scott Thompson, Ed Horowitz)

BENJI: OFF THE LEASH! (2004; CREDITS: Producer: Mulberry Square Productions; Director: Joe Camp; Screenplay: Joe Camp)

LASSIE (2005; CREDITS: Producer: Odyssey Entertainment Ltd,. Firstsight Films, Isle of Man Films, Ltd., Davis Films, Element Films, Elemental Films, Classic Media Productions; Director: Charles Sturridge; Screenplay: Charles Sturridge and Eric Knight (novel))

EIGHT BELOW (2006; CREDITS: Producer: Walt Disney Pictures; Director: Frank Marshall; Screenplay: Dave DiGilio, Koregoshi Kurahara, Tatsuo Nogami, Toshiro Ishido, Kan Saji)

FIREHOUSE DOG (2007; CREDITS: Producer: C.O.R.E. Digital Pictures/ New Regency Pictures; Director: Todd Holland; Screenplay: Claire-Dee Lim, Mike Werb)

FINDING RIN-TIN-TIN (2007; CREDITS: Producer: Emmet/Furla Films/New Image; Director: Danny Lerner, Jim Tierney; Screenplay: David Rolland)

COMPANIES OFFERING VIDEOTAPES AND DVDS OF SOME FILMS DISCUSSED IN THIS BOOK

amazon.com

Alpha
http://www.oldies.com

Discount Video Tapes (Hollywood's Attic)
P. O. Box 7122
Burbank, CA 91510
Telephone (818) 843-3366
http://www.hollywoodsattic.com

Facets Multimedia
1517 West Fullerton Avenue
Chicago, IL 60614
sales@facets.org

Forgotten Films: Rare and Hard To Find Movies
www.forgottenfilms.biz

Grapevine Video
4021 West San Juan Avenue
Phoenix, AZ 85019
http://www.grapevinevideo.com

Image Entertainment
20525 Nordhoff Street Suite 200
Chatsworth, CA 91311
inquiries@image-entertainment.com

Kino Intenational
333 W. 39th Street
New York, New York 10019
www.kino.com/video

Life Is A Movie
3639 Midway Drive B-326
San Diego, CA 92110
http://www.lifeisamovie.com

Movies Unlimited
3015 Darnell Road
Philadelphia, PA 19104
www.moviesunlimited.com

Satellite Media Production
P. O. Box 638
Walkersville, MD 27193^0638
www.oldietv.com

Sinister Cinema
P. O. Box 4369
Medford, Oregon
http://www.sinistercinema.com

VCI Entertainment
http://www.vcihomevideo.com

NOTES

Chapter 1

1. Burt, 17.

2. Jones, 1.

3. *Associated Press* (*Chicago Sun Times*), January 2, 2005.

4. *New York Daily News*, August 26, 2005.

5. *Imaginews*, 5.

6. Trimble, 10.

7. Ibid, 11.

8. *The New York Times*, January 20, 1922.

9. *The New York Times*, May 7, 1924.

10. Trimble, 19.

11. *Variety*, October 26, 1927.

12. Guldin, personal communication.

13. Denlinger, 43.

14. Brown, personal communication.

15. Kann (1928), 201.

16. Boone, 25.

Chapter 2

1. Hirshhorn, 42.

2. Foglesong, 92.

3. Ibid, 94.

4. Hall, *The New York Times*, November 25, 1924.

5. Dreyer v. Cyriacks 112 Cal.App. 279, 297 P. 35 (Cal.App. 1 Dist., Feb. 28, 1931).

6. Condon, 3.

7. *Box Office Record*, 196-209.

8. Kann (1927), 121.

9. Guldin, personal communication.

10. *The New York Times*, November 26, 1927.

11. Condon, 3.

12. Merghetti, 70.

13. Guldin, personal communication.

14. Ibid.

Chapter 3

1. Duncan, 43.

2. Thornton and Parker, 185.

3. Shields, 122.

4. Kiff, et al., 2.

5. Hirshhorn, 43.

6. Uncredited reviewer, *The New York Times*, December 26, 1929.

7. Condon, 2.

8. Fernett, 182.

9. Duncan, 73.

10. Hereford, 6

11. Houtsnede Maatchappij, 5.

12. Eder, *The New York Times*, May 27, 1976.

Chapter 4

1. Alicoate, 139.

2. Weiler, *The New York Times*, January 26, 1945.

3. Gammill, 3.

4. Malcolmson, 8.

5. Ibid, 91.

6. Young, 2.

Chapter 5

1. Weatherwax, 2.

2. Ibid, 3.

3. *Weiler, The New York Times*, June 11, 1945.

4. Young, 14.

5. Lemire, *The Associated Press*, September 1, 2006.

Chapter 6

1. Camp, 2.
2. Ibid, 3.
3. Weatherwax, 3.
4. Camp, 5.
5. Holden, *The New York Times*, April 28, 1989.
6. Maslin, *The New York Times*, April 17, 1992.

Chapter 7

1. Amaral, 11.
2. Burt, 153-154.

Chapter 8

1. Weiler, *The New York Times*, June 27, 1975.
2. Camp, 3.
3. Marshall, personal communication.

BIBLIOGRAPHY

Alicoate, Jack. Editor. *The Film Daily 1933 Year Book.* John W. Alicoate-Publishers, Ambassador Hotel, Los Angeles 1932.

Amaral, Anthony. *Movie Horses, Their Treatment and Training.* The Bobbs-Merrill Publishing Company, Incorporated, Indianapolis and New York, 1967.

Bergan, Ronald. *The United Artists Story.* Octopus Books, Limited/Crown Publisher, London, 1988.

Boone, J. Allen. *Kinship With All Life.* Harper & Row, Publishers, New York, Evanston and London, 1954.

_____. *Letters To Strongheart.* Prentice-Hall, Incorporated, New York, 1940.

Box Office Record: The Motion Picture Almanac. Quigley Publishing Company, 1929. pp. 196-209.

Brown, Lance. Personal communication.

Burt, Jonathan. *Animals In Film.* Reaktion Books Limited, London, 2002.

California Appellate Court, Dreyer v. Cyriacks 112 Cal.App. 279, 297 P. 35 (Cal.App. 1 Dist., Feb. 28, 1931).

Camp, Joe. *Benji Returns Website.* http://www.benjireturns.com

Condon, Dan. *Bugga C's Home Page.* http://home.comcast.net/~buggartt/

Denlinger, Milo G. *The Complete German Shepherd Third Edition.* Howell Book House, Incorporated, New York, 1961.

Dog Bite Law website. http://www.dogbitelaw.com

Duncan, Lee. *The Rin-Tin-Tin Book Of Dog Care.* Houghton-Mifflin and Company, New York, 1958.

DVD Verdict Review, *Lassie* (1994), in http://www.dvdverdict.com

Edelson, Edward. *Great Animals of The Movies.* Doubleday and Company, Garden City, New York 1980.

Eder, Richard. "Won Ton Ton, The Dog Who Saved Hollywood," review of *Won Ton Ton, The Dog Who Saved Hollywood, The New York Times*, May 27, 1976.

Eisenmann, Charles. *A Dog's Day In Court.* Eisenmann Books, 1589 NW Martin Avenue, Roseburg, Oregon 97470.

Fernett, Gene. *American Film Studios, An Historical Encyclopedia.* McFarland and Company, Incorporated, Publishers. Jefferson, North Carolina and London. 1988.

Foglesong, Clara M. *Peter.* Myne Publishing Company, Hollywood, California, 1945.

Gammill, Kerry. "Monster's Best Friend: Lon's Pal, Moose," *Monster Kid #* 1, online magazine issue dated 2001, at http://gammillustrations.bizland.com/

Guldin, Jere. Personal communication.

Hall, Mordaunt. "A New Dog Star," review of *The Silent Accuser*. *The New York Times*, November 25, 1924.

_____"Mr. Barrymore's New Idea," review of *The Thirteenth Hour*, *The New York Times*, November 26, 1927.

Hereford, Daphne. *Rinty's News*, a publication of the Rin-Tin-Tin Fan Club/ARF Kids Foundation, Incorporated. Website: http://www.rintintin.com

Hirshhorn, Clive. *The Warner Bros. Story*. Octopus Books Limited, London; Crown Publishers, New York 1980.

Holden, Stephen. "Pooch On Patrol," review of *K-9* in *The New York Times*, April 28, 1989.

Horton, Robert. "Lassie Comes Home to the Multiplexes," a review of *Lassie* in *The Herald* (Everett, Washington), September 1, 2006.

Houtsnede Maatschappij, N. V. Paramount Press book and Merchandising Manual, Won Ton Ton The Dog Who Saved Hollywood. Houtsnede Maatschappij, N. V. 1976.

The Internet Movie Database, http://www.imdb.com

Jones, Susan D. *From War Heroes to Priceless Pets: the Twentieth-Century American Dog*. Doctoral Dissertation. College of Liberal Arts, California Polytechnic State University, San Luis Obispo, California, 2003.

Kann, Maurice D. Editor. *The Film Daily 1928 Year Book*. John W. Alicoate-Publishers, Ambassador Hotel, Los Angeles 1927.

Kann, Maurice D. Editor. *The Film Daily 1929 Year Book*. John W. Alicoate Publishers, Ambassador Hotel, Los Angeles 1928.

Kiff, Lloyd F., Robert I. Mesta and Michael P. Wallace. *U. S. Fish and Wildlife Service Recovery Plan for the California Condor. April 1996, Third Revision*. U. S. Fish and Wildlife Service Region I, Portland, Oregon.

Kinney, Pamela. Personal communication.

Lemire, Christy. "Get out the hankies, 'Lassie' comes home again," a review of *Lassie*, *The Associated Press*, September 1, 2006.

Malcolmson, David. London: the Dog Who Made The Team. Duell, Sloan and Pearce, New York 1963.

Marshall, Debra. Personal communication.

Maslin, Janet. "Doggie Antics on Film," review of *Beethoven*, *The New York Times*, April 17, 1992.

Mereghetti, Paolo, Editor. *Dizionario dei film*. Baldoni and Castoldi Publishers, Italy, 1998.

Shields, Allan. *The Spirit of Rin-Tin-Tin*. Allan Shields, 2444 Beverly Avenue, Clovis, California, 93611, 2001. 183 pages.

The Silent Era website, http://www.silentera.com

Thornton, Kim Campbell, and Virginia Parker Guidry. *For The Love of Dogs*. Publications International Limited, Lincolnwood, Illinois, 1997.

Trimble, Lawrence. *Strongheart, The Story of a Wonder Dog*. Whitman Publishing Company, Racine, Wisconsin 1926.

Uncredited author, Lawrence Trimble biography, *Imaginenews*, http://www.imaginenews.com/Archives/2000/Mar_2000/Text/FEAT06.html

Uncredited reviewer. "Clash of the Wolves," review of *Clash of the Wolves*, Picture *Play Magazine*, February 1926

Uncredited reviewer. "The Night Cry," review of *The Night Cry*, *Picture Play Magazine*, July 1926.

Uncredited reviewer. "The Return of Boston Blackie," review of *The Return of Boston Blackie*. *Variety*, October 26, 1927.

Uncredited reviewer. "Strongheart Again," review of *The Love Master*. *The New York Times*, May 7, 1924.

Uncredited reviewer. untitled review of *The Silent Call*, *The New York Times*, January 20, 1922.

Uncredited reviewer. "'Tiger Rose' Opens The Beacon Theatre," review of *Tiger Rose*, *The New York Times*, December 26, 1929.

Uncredited author, "In And Out of Focus." *Motion Picture Magazine* Volume XXXV, Number 5, June 1928.

Weatherwax, Richard. *Weatherwax Dogs and The Movies website*. http://www.home.alt.net/~weatherwax/

Weiler, A. W. "At Loew's Criterion," review of *Son of Lassie*. *The New York Times*, June 11, 1945.

_____. "Benji," review of Benji. *The New York Times*, June 27, 1975.

_____. "The Thin Man Goes Home," review of *The Thin Man Goes Home*. *The New York Times*, January 26, 1945.

White, Michael. "'Saint' of cats dies." *The New York Daily News*, August 26, 2005.

Wittwer, Kathy. Personal communication.

Young, Linda. *The Unofficial Lassie Website*. http://www.flyingdreams.org/tv/lassie/lassmain.com

INDEX

If you enjoyed this book,
check out our other
film-related titles at
www.midmar.com
or call or write for a free catalog.
Midnight Marquee Press, Inc.
9721 Britinay Lane
Baltimore, MD 21234
410-665-1198
(8 a.m. until 6 p.m. EST)
or MMarquee@aol.com